D0915660

KIERKEGAARD

OUTSTANDING CHRISTIAN THINKERS

Series Editor: Brian Davies OP

The series offers a range of authoritative studies on people who have made an outstanding contribution to Christian thought and understanding. The series will range across the full spectrum of Christian thought to include Catholic and Protestant thinkers, to cover East and West, historical and contemporary figures. By and large, each volume will focus on a single 'thinker', but occasionally the subject may be a movement or a school of thought.

Brian Davies OP, the Series Editor, is Professor of Philosophy at Fordham University, New York. He was formerly Regent of Blackfriars, Oxford University, and Tutor in Theology at St Benet's Hall, Oxford University. He has taught at Bristol University, Emory University, and the Beda College in Rome. He is Reviews Editor of *International Philosophical Quarterly*. His previous publications include: *Thinking About God* (Geoffrey Chapman, 1985); *The Thought of Thomas Aquinas* (Oxford University Press, 1992); *An Introduction to the Philosophy of Religion* (revised edn, Oxford University Press, 1993); and he was editor of *Language, Meaning and God* (Geoffrey Chapman, 1987).

KIERKEGAARD

Julia Watkin

GEOFFREY
CHAPMAN

Geoffrey Chapman
A Cassell imprint
Wellington House, 125 Strand, London WC2R 0BB
127 West 24th Street, New York, NY 10011

© Julia Watkin 1997

First published 1997

British Library Cataloguing-in-Publication Data
A catalogue record for this book is available from the British Library.

ISBN 0–225–66815–7 (hardback)
0–225–66816–5 (paperback)

Typeset by Keystroke, Jacaranda Lodge, Wolverhampton
Printed and bound in Great Britain by
Biddles Ltd, Guildford and King's Lynn

Contents

tilegnet

Grethe Kjær

Editorial foreword

St Anselm of Canterbury once described himself as someone with faith seeking understanding. In words addressed to God he says 'I long to understand in some degree thy truth, which my heart believes and loves. For I do not seek to understand that I may believe, but I believe in order to understand.'

And this is what Christians have always inevitably said, either explicitly or implicitly. Christianity rests on faith, but it also has content. It teaches and proclaims a distinctive and challenging view of reality. It naturally encourages reflection. It is something to think about; something about which one might even have second thoughts.

But what have the greatest Christian thinkers said? And is it worth saying? Does it engage with modern problems? Does it provide us with a vision to live by? Does it make sense? Can it be preached? Is it believable?

This series originates with questions like these in mind. Written by experts, it aims to provide clear, authoritative and critical accounts of outstanding Christian writers from New Testament times to the present. It will range across the full spectrum of Christian thought to include Catholic and Protestant thinkers, thinkers from East and West, thinkers ancient, mediaeval and modern.

The series draws on the best scholarship currently available, so it will interest all with a professional concern for the history of Christian ideas. But contributors will also be writing for general readers who have little or no previous knowledge of the subjects to be dealt with. Volumes to appear should therefore prove helpful at a popular as well as an academic level. For the most part they will be devoted to a single thinker, but occasionally the subject will be a movement or school of thought.

Until the beginning of the twentieth century, the subject of the present volume was practically unknown outside his native Scandinavia. Yet, though interpretations of him have varied, he has proved to be a source of inspiration for numerous major theologians and philosophers (figures such as Martin Heidegger, Karl Jaspers, Karl Barth, Rudolf Bultmann and Paul Tillich), and his writings are now widely acknowledged to be a landmark in the history of Christian thinking. They range across some of the most important questions raised by Christianity, considered both as a set of teachings and as a way of life. And their treatment of these questions is original, powerful and always engaging. As the author of the present volume demonstrates, Kierkegaard is also a figure of contemporary interest, for he can be hailed as someone able to address undogmatically a variety of interests in a way that enables him to be viewed as a truly ecumenical figure in a pluralistic age.

Anyone writing an authoritative introduction to Kierkegaard must be expert in a number of fields. Dr Julia Watkin, the author of what follows, is someone to whom students of Kierkegaard can turn with confidence. As well as being thoroughly familiar with the language in which he wrote, she has been reading, thinking, teaching and writing about him for many years. She is a gifted theologian in her own right and she enjoys an international reputation as a Kierkegaard scholar. Her volume should establish itself as one of the most engaging and useful studies of its subject matter. As well as being a first-class introduction to those approaching Kierkegaard for the first time, it is also an impressively defended reading of Kierkegaard, one which will be welcomed by experts as well as beginners.

Brian Davies OP

Preface

I think I first encountered Kierkegaard's name as a child, as a silent listener to a philosophical discussion between my father, E. I. Watkin, and a Devonshire artist, Frank B. Lynch. Certainly there was a copy of Kierkegaard's *The Sickness unto Death* on the shelves of my nursery (really part of my father's library). The next time I heard the name I was a 24-year-old student standing outside the Church of St Mary-le-Strand in London in the spring of 1969, jotting down notes in an all-purpose notebook during a conversation with an informative fellow student. Under 'Kierkegaard' I noted: 'shows the final decision or commitment to Christianity as "a leap into the dark" (Existentialist).' There then (I shudder to say) follow further notes in connection with Kierkegaard, on 'Existentialism' as 'subjective ethics' (in the sense of self-invented), in which the names of Jean-Paul Sartre, Heidegger and Fellini appear. After that, Kierkegaard was forgotten until a decisive encounter with him as an undergraduate at Bristol University, where Dr (later Professor) John Kent, who regularly and spectacularly filleted the big names in religious studies like so many fish, manifesting their internal contradictions and weaknesses, was strangely lenient with Kierkegaard, thus arousing my curiosity and expectancy. This expectancy was not disappointed, since when I began to read Kierkegaard in 1972 I saw in a flash of illumination that I was encountering a great mind that had something to say to the problems of our time, and, most importantly for me, something to say to the twentieth-century crisis of religious belief. Nor was I alone in my enthusiasm, since I had the privilege of wonderful discussions on Kierkegaard with fellow students John Norris and Alan Keightley. Now, more than 20 years later, with Kierkegaard as constant companion, I see ever more clearly his importance as one able to raise and address vital philosophical and ethical-religious questions about existence, raise them in such a way that his thought must be relevant to every generation. Surely few can be read so widely and avidly on both an interdisciplinary and an international basis. I am happy to count myself one of his readers and grateful for the opportunity to write about him in this series where he truly belongs.

My grateful thanks to Stephen Evans for acting as reading consultant for this book, to series editor Brian Davies, also to Grethe Kjær, especially for her helpful critical comments and support during the period of writing that began in Copenhagen and ended in Tasmania.

Julia Watkin
April 1996

Abbreviations and bibliography

Abbreviations come first, listed in alphabetical order. Bibliography titles are listed under: Danish books, author surname order; English books, author surname order; Articles, and General Kierkegaard bibliographies, author surname order (or journal title where relevant). With a few exceptions, references to Kierkegaard's works (as well as to his papers) are to the Danish editions (followed by the abbreviation of the relevant English translation), since Danish pagination is provided in translations of his Collected Works.

ABBREVIATIONS

AC Søren Kierkegaard, *Kierkegaard's Attack Upon 'Christendom'* (Princeton, NJ: Princeton University Press, 1968).

AN Søren Kierkegaard, *Armed Neutrality and an Open Letter* (Bloomington and London: Indiana University Press, 1968; Clarion, Simon and Schuster, 1969).

BALLE Nikolai Edinger Balle, *Lærebog i den Evangelisk-christelige Religion indrettet til Brug i de danske Skoler* (Copenhagen: Jens Hostrup Schultz, 1849).

CA Søren Kierkegaard, *The Concept of Anxiety: Kierkegaard's Writings* (Princeton, NJ: Princeton University Press, 1980).

CD Søren Kierkegaard, *Christian Discourses* (Princeton, NJ: Princeton University Press, 1940, 1971).

CI Søren Kierkegaard, *The Concept of Irony: Kierkegaard's Writings* (Princeton, NJ: Princeton University Press, 1989).

COR Søren Kierkegaard, *The Corsair Affair: Kierkegaard's Writings* (Princeton, NJ: Princeton University Press, 1982).

CUP Søren Kierkegaard, *Concluding Unscientific Postscript: Kierkegaard's Writings* (Princeton, NJ: Princeton University Press, 1992), I.

EOI Søren Kierkegaard, *Either/Or Part I: Kierkegaard's Writings* (Princeton, NJ: Princeton University Press, 1987).

EOII Søren Kierkegaard, *Either/Or Part II*: *Kierkegaard's Writings* (Princeton, NJ: Princeton University Press, 1987).

EPW Søren Kierkegaard, *Early Polemical Writings*: *Kierkegaard's Writings* (Princeton, NJ: Princeton University Press, 1990).

EUD Søren Kierkegaard, *Eighteen Upbuilding Discourses*: *Kierkegaard's Writings* (Princeton, NJ: Princeton University Press, 1990).

FSE/JY Søren Kierkegaard, *For Self-Examination/Judge For Yourself!*: *Kierkegaard's Writings* (Princeton, NJ: Princeton University Press, 1990).

FS-JY Søren Kierkegaard, *For Self-Examination and Judge For Yourselves!* (Princeton, NJ: Princeton University Press, 1941, 1968).

FT/R Søren Kierkegaard, *Fear and Trembling/Repetition*: *Kierkegaard's Writings* (Princeton, NJ: Princeton University Press, 1983).

JP Howard and Edna Hong (eds), *Søren Kierkegaard's Journals and Papers* (Bloomington and London: Indiana University Press, 1967–78).

LD Søren Kierkegaard, *Letters and Documents*: *Kierkegaard's Writings* (Princeton, NJ: Princeton University Press, 1978).

OAR Søren Kierkegaard, *On Authority and Revelation* (New York: Harper Torchbook edn, Harper & Row, 1966).

PA Søren Kierkegaard, *The Present Age and Two Minor Ethico-Religious Treatises* (London: Oxford University Press, 1940).

PAP Søren Kierkegaard, *Papirer* I–XIII (2nd edn; Copenhagen: P. A. Heiberg, V. Kuhr, E. Torsting, Niels Thulstrup (index XIV–XVI, N.-J. Cappelørn), Gyldendal, 1968–78).

PC Søren Kierkegaard, *Practice in Christianity*: *Kierkegaard's Writings* (Princeton, NJ: Princeton University Press, 1991).

PF Søren Kierkegaard, *Philosophical Fragments/Johannes Climacus*: *Kierkegaard's Writings* (Princeton, NJ: Princeton University Press, 1985).

PVMA Søren Kierkegaard, *The Point of View for My Work as An Author: A Report to History* (Harper Torchbook edn; New York: Harper & Row, 1962).

SD Søren Kierkegaard, *The Sickness unto Death*: *Kierkegaard's Writings* (Princeton, NJ: Princeton University Press, 1980).

SLW Søren Kierkegaard, *Stages on Life's Way*: *Kierkegaard's Writings* (Princeton, NJ: Princeton University Press, 1988).

SV Søren Kierkegaard, *Samlede Værker* I–XIV (1st edn; Copenhagen: A. B. Drachmann, J. L. Heiberg, H. O. Lange,

Gyldendalske Boghandels Forlag, 1901–06).

TA Søren Kierkegaard, *Two Ages: Kierkegaard's Writings* (Princeton, NJ: Princeton University Press, 1978).

UDVS Søren Kierkegaard, *Upbuilding Discourses in Various Spirits: Kierkegaard's Writings* (Princeton, NJ: Princeton University Press, 1993).

WL Søren Kierkegaard, *Works of Love: Kierkegaard's Writings* (Princeton, NJ: Princeton University Press, 1995).

BIBLIOGRAPHY

Danish books

Villads Ammundsen, *Søren Kierkegaards Ungdom* (Copenhagen: Universitetsbogtrykkeriet, 1912).

H. P. Barfod, *Til Minde om Biskop Peter Christian Kierkegaard* (Copenhagen: Karl Schønbergs Forlag, 1888).

Birgit Bertung, Paul Müller and Fritz Norlan (eds), *Kierkegaard Pseudonymitet: Søren Kierkegaard Selskabets Populære Skrifter* XXI (Copenhagen: C. A. Reitzels Forlag, 1993).

Leif Bork Hansen, *Søren Kierkegaards Hemmelighed og Eksistensdialektik* (Copenhagen: C. A. Reitzels Forlag, 1994).

H. N. Clausen, *Catholicismens og Protestantismens Kirkeforfatning, Lære og Ritus* (Copenhagen: Andreas Seidelin, 1825).

N. F. S. Grundtvig, *Kirkens Gienmæle* (Copenhagen: 1825).

Johan Ludvig Heiberg, *Om Philosophiens Betydning for den Nuværende Tid* (Copenhagen: 1833).

Kjeld Holm, Malthe Jacobsen and Bjarne Troelsen (eds), *Søren Kierkegaard og Romantikerne* (Copenhagen: Berlingske Forlag, 1974).

Otto Holmgaard, *Peter Christian Kierkegaard* (Copenhagen: Rosenkilde og Bagger, 1953).

Steen Johansen, *Erindringer om Søren Kierkegaard* (Copenhagen: C. A. Reitzels Boghandel, 1980).

Grethe Kjær, *Den Gådefulde Familie* (Copenhagen: C. A. Reitzels Boghandel, 1981).

Grethe Kjær, *Søren Kierkegaards seks optegnelser om den Store Jordrystelse* (Copenhagen: C. A. Reitzels Forlag, 1983).

Grethe Kjær, *Barndommens ulykkelige Elsker* (Copenhagen: C. A. Reitzels Forlag, 1986).

Carl Koch, *Søren Kierkegaard og Emil Boesen* (Copenhagen: Karl Schønbergs Forlag, 1901).

Carl Henrik Koch, *En Flue på Hegels Udødelige Næse* (Copenhagen: C. A. Reitzels Forlag, 1990).

Sejer Kühle, *Søren Kierkegaard: Barndom og Ungdom* (Copenhagen: Aschenhoug Dansk Forlag, 1950).

Olof G. Lidin, *Japans Religioner* (Copenhagen: Politikens Forlag, 1985).

Valter Lindström, *Stadiernas Teologi* (Lund and Copenhagen: Gleerup & Gad, 1943).

Henriette Lund, *Erindringer fra Hjemmet* (Copenhagen: Gyldendalske Boghandel Nordisk Forlag, 1909).

K. E. Løgstrup, *Den Etiske Fordring* (Copenhagen: Gyldendal, 1956, 1975).

K. E. Løgstrup, *Opgør med Kierkegaard* (Copenhagen: Gyldendal, 1968, 1994).

Gregor Malantschuk, *Nøglebegreber i Søren Kierkegaards tænkning* (ed. Grethe Kjær and Paul Müller; Copenhagen: C. A. Reitzels Forlag, 1993).

Hans Lassen Martensen, *Af mit Levnet* I–III (Copenhagen: Gyldendalske Boghandels Forlag, 1882–83).

Jakob P. Mynster, *Prædikener paa alle Søn- og Hellig-Dage i Aaret* (Copenhagen: Gyldendalske Boghandlings Forlag, 1845).

Erik Pontoppidan, *Sandhed til Gudfrygtighed* (Stavanger: 1849).

H. Roos, *Søren Kierkegaard og Katolicismen: Søren Kierkegaard Selskabets Populære Skrifter* II (Copenhagen: Ejnar Munksgaard, 1952).

Poul Roubiczek, *Eksistentialismen: En kritisk vurdering* (Copenhagen: Munksgaard, 1968).

Svend Erik Stybe, *Universitet og Åndsliv i 500 År* (Copenhagen: G. E. C. Gad, 1979).

Marie Mikulová Thulstrup, *Kierkegaard og Pietismen: Søren Kierkegaard Selskabets Populære Skrifter* XIII (Copenhagen: Munksgaards Forlag, 1967).

Niels Thulstrup (ed.), *Breve og Aktstykker vedrørende Søren Kierkegaard* I–II (Copenhagen: Munksgaard, 1953–54).

Niels Thulstrup, *Kierkegaards Forhold til Hegel* (Copenhagen: Gyldendal, 1967).

Carl Weltzer, *Peter og Søren Kierkegaard* (Copenhagen: G. E. C. Gads Forlag, 1936).

English books

Sylviane Agacinski, *Aparté: Conceptions and Deaths of Søren Kierkegaard* (Tallahassee: Florida State University Press, 1986).

George E. and George B. Arbaugh, *Kierkegaard's Authorship* (London: George Allen and Unwin, 1968).

Peter Atkins, *Creation Revisited* (London: Penguin Books, 1992).

Donald Attwater (ed.), *The Catholic Encyclopædic Dictionary* (2nd revised edn; London: Cassell, 1949).

Emil Brunner, *Truth as Encounter* (Philadelphia: Westminster, 1964).

Albert Camus, *The Myth of Sisyphus* (London: Penguin Books, 1988).

John D. Caputo, *Radical Hermeneutics: Repetition, Deconstruction, and the Hermeneutic Project* (Bloomington and Indianapolis: Indiana University Press, 1987).

Paul M. Churchland, *Matter and Consciousness* (Cambridge, MA/ Bradford: The MIT Press, 1993).

T. H. Croxall, *Glimpses and Impressions of Kierkegaard* (London: James Nisbet & Co. Ltd., 1959).

Don Cupitt, *The Sea of Faith* (London: British Broadcasting Corporation, 1984).

Elmer H. Duncan, *Søren Kierkegaard* (Waco, TX: Word Books, 1976).

Louis Dupré, *Kierkegaard as Theologian* (London and New York: Sheed & Ward, 1963).

C. Stephen Evans, *Kierkegaard's 'Fragments' and 'Postscript': The Religious Philosophy of Johannes Climacus* (Atlantic Highlands, NJ: Humanities Press, 1983).

C. Stephen Evans, *Passionate Reason: Making Sense of Kierkegaard's 'Philosophical Fragments'* (Bloomington and Indianapolis: Indiana University Press, 1992).

Henning Fenger, *Kierkegaard: The Myths and Their Origins* (New Haven: Yale University Press, 1980).

Patrick Gardiner, *Kierkegaard* (Oxford: Oxford University Press, 1988).

Henri Ghéon, *The Secret of Saint John Bosco* (London: Sheed & Ward, 1935).

Ronald Grimsley, *Kierkegaard* (London: Studio Vista, 1973).

Alastair Hannay, *Kierkegaard* (London: Routledge & Kegan Paul, 1982).

F. C. Happold, *Religious Faith and Twentieth-Century Man* (Harmondsworth: Penguin Books, 1966).

Aage Henriksen, *Methods and Results of Kierkegaard Studies in Scandinavia* (Copenhagen: Ejnar Munksgaard, 1951).

John Hick, *Death and Eternal Life* (London: Collins, 1976).

Craig Quentin Hinkson, 'Kierkegaard's theology: Cross and grace. The Lutheran and Idealist traditions in his thought' (Chicago: PhD in theology, University of Chicago Divinity School, December 1993).

Johannes Hohlenberg, *Sören Kierkegaard* (New York: Pantheon Books Inc., 1954; Octagon Books, 1978).

Aldous Huxley, *The Devils of Loudun* (New York: Carroll & Graf Publishers, Inc., 1986).

Karl Jaspers, *Philosophy* (Chicago: University of Chicago Press, 1969).

Niels Lyhne Jensen (ed.), *A Grundtvig Anthology* (Denmark and Cambridge: Centrum/James Clarke & Co., 1984).

Walter Kaufmann, *Existentialism From Dostoevsky to Sartre* (Cleveland and New York: Meridian Books, 1956).

John Kent, *The End of the Line?* (Philadelphia: Fortress Press, 1982).

Bruce Kirmmse, *Kierkegaard in Golden Age Denmark* (Indiana: Indiana University Press, 1990).

R. D. Laing, *The Divided Self* (Harmondsworth: Penguin Books, 1965, 1969).

David R. Law, *Kierkegaard as Negative Theologian* (Oxford: Clarendon Press, 1993).

C. S. Lewis, *The Abolition of Man* (London and Glasgow: Collins Fount Paperbacks, 1984).

Timothy Tian Min Lin, *The Life and Thought of Søren Kierkegaard* (New Haven, CT: College & University Press, 1974).

P. G. Lindhardt, *Grundtvig: An Introduction* (London: SPCK, 1951).

Walter Lowrie, *Kierkegaard* (London: Oxford University Press, 1938).

Walter Lowrie, *A Short Life of Kierkegaard* (London: Humphrey Milford/Oxford University Press, 1944).

Louis Mackey, *Points of View: Readings of Kierkegaard* (Tallahassee: Florida State University Press, 1986).

John Macquarrie, *Twentieth-Century Religious Thought* (London: SCM Press, 1963, 1976).

Gregor Malantschuk, *Kierkegaard's Way to the Truth* (Minneapolis: Augsburg Publishing House, 1963; Montreal: Inter Editions, 1987).

Gregor Malantschuk, *Kierkegaard's Thought* (Princeton, NJ: Princeton University Press, 1971).

Hans Lassen Martensen, *Christian Dogmatics* (Edinburgh: T. & T. Clark, 1871).

Hans Lassen Martensen, *Christian Ethics* (Edinburgh: T. & T. Clark, 1881–82).

Edward F. Mooney, *Knights of Faith and Resignation: Reading Kierkegaard's 'Fear and Trembling'* (Albany, NY: State University of New York Press, 1991).

Robert L. Perkins (ed.), *Kierkegaard's 'Fear and Trembling': Critical Appraisals* (Alabama: The University of Alabama Press, 1981).

Robert L. Perkins (ed.), *International Kierkegaard Commentary: 'Fear and Trembling' and 'Repetition'* (Macon, GA: Mercer University Press, 1993).

Revised English Bible with Apocrypha (Oxford: Oxford University Press/Cambridge: Cambridge University Press, 1989).

Peter Rohde, *Søren Kierkegaard* (London: Allen & Unwin Ltd, 1963).

Paul Roubiczek, *Existentialism: For and Against* (Cambridge: Cambridge University Press, 1964).

Jean-Paul Sartre, *Existentialism and Humanism* (London: Methuen & Co. Ltd, 1948).

Peter Singer, *Hegel* (Oxford: Oxford University Press, 1983).

Johannes Sløk, *Kierkegaard's Universe: A New Guide to the Genius* (Copenhagen: The Danish Cultural Institute, 1994).

Svend Erik Stybe, *Copenhagen University 500 Years of Science and Scholarship* (Copenhagen: The Royal Danish Ministry of Foreign Affairs, 1979).

Mark C. Taylor, *Kierkegaard's Pseudonymous Authorship: A Study of Time and the Self* (Princeton, NJ: Princeton University Press, 1975).

Reidar Thomte, *Kierkegaard's Philosophy of Religion* (Princeton, NJ: Princeton University Press, 1948; Greenwood Press reprint, 1969).

Niels Thulstrup, *Kierkegaard's Relation to Hegel* (Princeton, NJ: Princeton University Press, 1980).

Niels Thulstrup and Marie Mikulová Thulstrup (eds), *Bibliotheca*

Kierkegaardiana I–XVI (Copenhagen: C. A. Reitzels Boghandel & Forlag, 1978–88).

Paul Tillich, *Perspectives on 19th and 20th Century Protestant Theology*, ed. Carl R. Braaten (New York: Harper & Row, 1967).

Paul Tillich, *Systematic Theology* (Great Britain: James Nisbet & Co., 1968).

Renate Wind, *A Spoke in the Wheel: The Life of Dietrich Bonhoeffer* (London: SCM Press, 1991).

Clifton Wolters (tr.), *The Cloud of Unknowing and Other Works* (Harmondsworth: Penguin Books, 1961, 1978).

J. A. Ziesler, *Christian Asceticism* (London: SPCK, 1973).

Articles

Karl Barth, 'A thank you and a bow: Kierkegaard's reveille', *Canadian Journal of Theology* 11 (1965), 1, pp. 3–7.

Safet Bektovic, 'Kierkegaard og Islam', *Information*, Copenhagen, 2–3 (1994), April.

John Biermans, Michael Giampaoli and others, 'Profile of Rev. Moon's life', *New Vision for World Peace* (Chung H. Kwak, Holy Spirit Association for the Unification of World Christianity, 1988), pp. 57–64.

Jørgen K. Bukdahl, 'Bultmann' in Niels Thulstrup and Marie Mikulová Thulstrup (eds), *Bibliotheca Kierkegaardiana* VIII: *The Legacy and Interpretation of Kierkegaard* (Copenhagen: C. A. Reitzels Boghandel, 1981), pp. 238–42.

Newsweek, 'Last days of the Waco cult – death wish', 3 May 1993, pp. 10–17.

Jørgen Pedersen, 'Augustine and Augustinianism' in Niels Thulstrup and Marie Mikulová Thulstrup (eds), *Bibliotheca Kierkegaardiana* VI: *Kierkegaard and Great Traditions* (Copenhagen: C. A. Reitzels Boghandel, 1981), pp. 54–97.

Robert L. Perkins, 'A philosophic encounter with Buber' in Niels Thulstrup and Marie Mikulová Thulstrup (eds), *Bibliotheca Kierkegaardiana* VIII: *The Legacy and Interpretation of Kierkegaard* (Copenhagen: C. A. Reitzels Boghandel, 1981), pp. 243–75.

Regin Prenter, 'Luther and Lutheranism' in Niels Thulstrup and Marie Mikulová Thulstrup (eds), *Bibliotheca Kierkegaardiana* VI: *Kierkegaard and Great Traditions* (Copenhagen: C. A. Reitzels Boghandel, 1981), pp. 121–73.

Johannes Sløk, 'Kierkegaard and Luther' in Howard A. Johnson and Niels Thulstrup (eds), *A Kierkegaard Critique* (New York: Harper & Brothers, 1962), ch. 6.

N. H. Søe, 'Karl Barth' in Niels Thulstrup and Marie Mikulová Thulstrup (eds), *Bibliotheca Kierkegaardiana* VIII: *The Legacy and Interpretation of Kierkegaard* (Copenhagen: C. A. Reitzels Boghandel, 1981), pp. 224–37.

Richard Summers, 'British Kierkegaard research: a historical survey', *Kierkegaardiana* 15 (1991), pp. 117–35.

Marie Mikulová Thulstrup, 'Pietism' in Niels Thulstrup and Marie Mikulová Thulstrup (eds), *Bibliotheca Kierkegaardiana* VI: *Kierkegaard and Great Traditions* (Copenhagen: C. A. Reitzels Boghandel, 1981), pp. 173–222.

Time, 'Cult of death', 4 December 1978, pp. 6–14.

Time, 'Tragedy in Waco', 3 May 1993, pp. 26–43.

Sylvia Walsh, 'Kierkegaard and postmodernism', *International Journal for Philosophy of Religion* 29 (1991), pp. 113–22.

Julia Watkin, 'The criteria of ethical-religious authority: Kierkegaard and Adolph Adler', *ACME – Annali della Facoltà di Lettere e Filosofia dell'Università degli Studi di Milano* 45.1 (January–April 1992), pp. 27–40.

Julia Watkin, 'The Journals and the Works of 1843 with particular reference to *Either/Or*', *Topicos: revista de filosofía* 3.5 (1993), pp. 19–51.

Julia Watkin, 'Judge William – a Christian?' in Robert L. Perkins (ed.), *International Kierkegaard Commentary: 'Either/Or II'* (Macon, GA: Mercer University Press, 1995), ch. 5.

General Kierkegaard bibliographies

Calvin D. Evans, *Søren Kierkegaard Bibliographies* (Montreal: McGill University Libraries, Fontanus Monograph Series, 1993).

Jun Hashimoto, Michimune Madenokoji and Takahiro Hirabayashi, *Søren Kierkegaard Litteratur i Japan (1906–1979), Bøger til 1994* (Nishinomiya, Japan: Kwansei Gakuin University, 1995).

Jens Himmelstrup, *International Kierkegaard Bibliografi* (Copenhagen: Nyt Nordisk Forlag/Arnold Busck, 1962).

International Kierkegaard Information (University of Tasmania: Internet, 1994).

Aage Jørgensen, *Søren Kierkegaard-litteratur 1961–1970* (Aarhus: Akademisk Boghandel, 1971).

Aage Jørgensen, 'Søren Kierkegaard-litteratur 1971–1980: en bibliografi', *Kierkegaardiana* 12 (1982), pp. 129–235.

Aage Jørgensen, *Søren Kierkegaard-litteratur 1971–1980* (Aarhus: 1983).

Aage Jørgensen and Stéphane Hogue, 'Søren Kierkegaard literature 1981–1991. A bibliography', *Kierkegaardiana* 16 (1993), pp. 166–239.

Aage Jørgensen, 'Søren Kierkegaard literature 1992–1993. A bibliography', *Kierkegaardiana* 17 (1994), pp. 221–36.

François H. Lapointe, *Sören Kierkegaard and His Critics: An International Bibliography of Criticism* (Westport, CT and London: Greenwood Press, 1980).

Julia Watkin, *International Kierkegaard Newsletter* (ISSN 0108–3104; 1979–).

Acknowledgements

Grateful acknowledgement for permission to quote is made to:

The Canadian Corporation for Studies in Religion, for Karl Barth, 'A thank you and a bow: Kierkegaard's reveille';

Indiana University Press, for *Søren Kierkegaard's Journals and Papers*, ed. and tr. Howard and Edna Hong;

Princeton University Press, for *Kierkegaard's Writings*, ed. Howard V. Hong; Kierkegaard, *On Authority and Revelation*, tr. Walter Lowrie; and *Kierkegaard's Attack Upon Christendom*, tr. Walter Lowrie;

The University of Chicago Press, for Karl Jaspers, *Philosophy*, 'Epilogue 1955';

Dr John Ziesler, for *Christian Asceticism*.

1

The approach to Kierkegaard

The twentieth-century world inherited from Søren Kierkegaard (1813–55) the legacy of a large and varied authorship that has been claimed and acclaimed by specialists in many fields. Due to the nature of his authorship,[1] however, and particularly to his methodology, Kierkegaard has often been interpreted and even misinterpreted in ways that have obscured the burning purpose of his writings entirely. His name has been linked with atheistic existentialism,[2] with a purely humanistic religiosity,[3] and not least with postmodernism,[4] all of which he would have criticized in different ways and for different reasons. Particularly unfortunate here are two tendencies that have appeared in Kierkegaard research. One is to treat him as if his life's dialogue was solely with outstanding philosophers and literary figures and the task to find his precise position in the stream of the history of ideas. The direction of the flow is then charted, often with Kierkegaard seen as radically affecting it as the 'Father of Existentialism', and an attempt is made to put later 'followers' in their proper place in the stream.[5] The other tendency concerns a mistaken chain of psychological inferences. The chain starts with two links: the recognition that Kierkegaard was a genius and the thought that we must in our own day know more about everything than people did in previous centuries. A connection is then made between the two links, namely that Kierkegaard the genius must have been in advance of his time and in a position to see a lot more truth than his contemporaries, and that therefore he could not have held traditional Christian perceptions of God and the world. This chain is then used to show that what Kierkegaard says himself about the authorship is simply Kierkegaard not being honest with himself and/or the reader. Alternatively, work is done on his language, so that there is imported into it a twentieth-century non-realist or atheistic understanding of his talk of God and Christianity.

It thus cannot be too strongly stressed that Kierkegaard was a Christian thinker and an outstanding one, believing in the God of traditional Christianity,[6] though it has to be recognized that he makes it difficult for the reader to see this because of his method of communication, his denial that he was a Christian (as he defined the word), and last, but not least, because of his presentation of Christianity, a presentation that in places resembles an attack.

This book will therefore introduce Kierkegaard the Christian thinker, but it must at the outset also attempt to deal with the question of interpretation and make clear its own methodology. Thus, in order to make proper contact with Kierkegaard, the ground will be cleared by my giving Kierkegaard's own personal and cultural background, followed by a presentation of his basic assumptions about the structure of the Christian universe and the development of his vocation as religious writer.[7] After this, a concise chapter on his writings will show why Kierkegaard is entirely different from others in his treatment of Christianity, for this is where his radicality lies. The path of exploration will then follow Kierkegaard's presentations of Christian ideality and the tension and opposition in his authorship between Christianity as godly enjoyment of the world and Christianity as renunciation and total self-denial. Particularly emphasized will be the connections between ethics and religion.

Part of the methodology is self-evident: a consideration of personal and cultural factors relevant to the life of Kierkegaard. More difficult is deciding how to deal with an authorship the half of which is under diverse pseudonyms and which Kierkegaard specifically asks us not to identify with his own personal viewpoint.[8] In short, how do I know exactly what Kierkegaard's own view of Christianity was, and how can one piece it together from such an authorship? The answer is, of course, that I cannot, in the sense of mathematical certainty, know exactly what anyone's view is, and one can never totally escape the problem of the borderline between acceptable and unacceptable explanations of anything. One can, however, decide what one finds to be the most acceptable explanation and why, and an important element here must be how well the explanation fits all the facts.[9] In this case, a key factor must be how far one decides to accept the validity of Kierkegaard's own explanations,[10] and after many years with Kierkegaard I still have no hesitation in accepting the overall tenor of what he says. While he clearly realizes creativity and development, both in himself and in the authorship, his claim that he is consciously a religious author firmly supports an understanding of his writings that causes the entire authorship to hang together in a well-connected whole.[11] My assessment of his writings does not depend solely on Kierkegaard's own explanations, however, but also on a careful consideration of sources, of the critics' objections, and finally of material that has never before to my knowledge been given its proper due.

As will become apparent, this book aims to present Kierke-gaard's thought distinctly and simply from a new angle so that it will additionally serve as an introduction for new readers. It will also quite deliberately avoid the traditional tramp through Kierkegaard's 'three stages', since, in my view, this approach tends to create unnecessary problems requiring explanation. In my presentation of Kierkegaard, I will deal with selected material that best illuminates the particular point at issue, aiming to put flesh on the framework of his Christian assumptions while showing the movement of his thought concerning Christianity as a way of life. Finally, it should be noted that although Kierkegaard is most emphatically a Christian religious thinker, writing at a particular time and for a particular culture, he also – because of his deep insights concerning life in an age of crisis – comes to speak to the many creeds and cultures in our modern world.

Notes

1. See Chapter 4. Kierkegaard gradually constructed a complex 'author-ship' (*Forfatterskab*) consisting of pseudonymous works and works under his own name. His pseudonyms were made to represent different standpoints.
2. E.g. Jean-Paul Sartre.
3. An example of this is to be found in the section on Kierkegaard in Don Cupitt, *The Sea of Faith* (London: British Broadcasting Corporation, 1984), pp. 146–56, esp. 153–4. Here Kierkegaard is seen as represent-ing a non-realist Christian position with Christianity demythologized into spirituality.
4. E.g. Sylviane Agacinski, *Aparté: Conceptions and Deaths of Søren Kierkegaard* (Tallahassee: Florida State University Press, 1986); John D. Caputo, *Radical Hermeneutics: Repetition, Deconstruction, and the Hermeneutic Project* (Bloomington and Indianapolis, Indiana University Press, 1987). Sylvia Walsh gives an excellent analysis of

postmodernism and Kierkegaard in 'Kierkegaard and post-modernism', *International Journal for Philosophy of Religion* 29 (1991), pp. 113–22.

5. This has proved particularly difficult with the presupposition that Kierkegaard is the 'Father of Existentialism'. Awkward problems arise; for example, the question of the relation of Dostoevsky to Kierkegaard (there was no contact between them) or of Albert Camus to Kierkegaard (he by no means 'followed' Kierkegaard, and does not appear to have understood him terribly well in his book *The Myth of Sisyphus* (London: Penguin Books, 1988), pp. 39–42). The practical difficulty of placing certain authors together as 'existentialists' is well illustrated by Walter Kaufmann's book *Existentialism From Dostoevsky to Sartre* (Cleveland and New York: Meridian Books, 1956) where, starting with Dostoevsky but ending in fact with Camus, the book clearly demonstrates the difficulties of placing the authors together, of finding genuine connections and likenesses.

6. Kierkegaard attaches his personal Christian belief to Jesus as God incarnate, and he also clearly believes in a transcendent God and eternal realm such that God and that realm would exist as fact even if there were no human beings. This does not mean, however, that he views either God or heaven as somehow materialistically linked to the ordinary spatio-temporal world.

7. Kierkegaard can of course be fruitfully presented as philosopher, psychologist or novelist, to name but three approaches, but he would have seen none of these as being the driving force behind his authorship.

8. See, e.g., SV, VII, pp. [545–9] (CUP), 'A first and last explanation'.

9. Of possible methods of approach to Kierkegaard can be named the biographical-psychological, the historical-comparative, the literary, and the thematic. See Aage Henriksen, *Methods and Results of Kierkegaard Studies in Scandinavia* (Copenhagen: Ejnar Munksgaard, 1951), pp. 7–12; Mark C. Taylor, *Kierkegaard's Pseudonymous Authorship: A Study of Time and the Self* (Princeton, NJ: Princeton University Press, 1975), pp. 18–37; David R. Law, *Kierkegaard as Negative Theologian* (Oxford: Clarendon Press, 1993), pp. 3–8. C. Stephen Evans, *Passionate Reason: Making Sense of Kierkegaard's 'Philosophical Fragments'* (Bloomington and Indianapolis: Indiana University Press, 1992), pp. 2–4, divides recent literature on Kierkegaard into three categories: a philosophical approach that emphasizes Kierkegaard as a philosopher and regards the particular character of the pseudonym as unimportant; a literary approach focusing attention on the literary form of Kierkegaard's works; and finally, a third category, literary-philosophical, which combines the other two approaches.

10. Here I am particularly thinking of his *About My Activity as a Writer* (1851) and the posthumously published *The Point of View for My Work as an Author* (1859), SV, XIII (PVMA), but there is also other relevant material in the authorship, not least in his Journals, PAP (JP).

11. I attempt to examine the problem of interpretation in my paper 'The Journals and the Works of 1843 with particular reference to *Either/Or*',

Topicos: revista de filosofía 3.5 (1993), pp. 19–51. I cannot see how extreme scepticism about Kierkegaard's personal honesty or his ability to state the truth does more than bring us to the brink of communication chaos, since one can take extreme scepticism to any lengths – also to the extent of doubting the extreme scepticism. For examples of sceptical views, see Henning Fenger, *Kierkegaard: The Myths and Their Origins* (New Haven: Yale University Press, 1980) and Louis Mackey, *Points of View: Readings of Kierkegaard* (Tallahassee: Florida State University Press, 1986).

2

Personal and cultural background

Paradoxically, Søren Kierkegaard lived at a time of stability and conflict, a stability and conflict that applied as much to his own home as to the surrounding world.[1] He belongs to Denmark's Golden Age (1800–70), an age that was stable enough to produce an unprecedented flowering in the arts and sciences.[2] Yet this age also saw dramatic transition from rural serfdom to the modern world, while there were a number of disasters due chiefly to Denmark's catastrophic entanglement in the Napoleonic wars.[3] The French Revolution of 27 July 1830 also led to political risings and disturbances throughout Europe, but Denmark remained politically stable despite the enormous transition from absolute to constitutional monarchy in 1849.[4] When we turn to the details of Kierkegaard's personal life, our attention is at once drawn to his unusual family background, where again one can see stability and conflict. Here, however, so much emphasis has been placed on Kierkegaard's relation to his father and on the isolating gloom caused by a family secret or secrets, that elements of the total picture tend to get misrepresented or even left out.[5] It is important, therefore, to give all elements their due, not least the religious contrasts and their relationship to the family's social background.

We can begin with the fact that both Kierkegaard's parents came from working-class farming families in Jutland.[6] Kierkegaard's mother, Anne Sørensdatter Lund (1768–1834), was a daughter of crofter Søren Jensen of Brandlund (hence the name Lund).[7] Anne's eldest brother Lars was already in Copenhagen when she became servant girl there, first to the sister-in-law before the marriage, then to cloth-merchant Mads Røyen, and finally to Mads' brother-in-law

Michael Pedersen Kierkegaard and his first wife Kirstine Niels-datter Røyen.[8] A year after the death of his first wife in 1796, Michael Kierkegaard married Anne, who gave birth to their first child Maren Kirstine not five months after the wedding on 26 April 1797. Much has been made of the fact that Michael apparently had to marry Anne because of the pregnancy, and of the fact that the marriage settlement was a poor one, envisaging the possibility of separation or divorce, but there is nothing to indicate that the marriage itself was unhappy. Within five years Michael drew up a will with good provision for his wife, and the epitaph on her grave indicates great affection.[9] While there is little material about Kierkegaard's mother, there is more than enough to show that claims[10] that she was regarded after marriage as an unimportant illiterate servant, and that she never figured in Kierkegaard's authorship, are not accurate. While Anne Kierkegaard could not write, it appears she could read.[11] Nor should too much emphasis be placed on her activity in serving her family when both Michael and Anne Kierkegaard were country working class and Michael himself from a background of poverty. Even though he became a rich man, Michael's daughters Nicoline and Petrea were, for a time, expected to do the work of servants in the home,[12] while Michael himself found nothing odd in regularly doing the shopping. In the only account we have of her,[13] Anne Kierkegaard is said to have been 'a nice little woman with a homely and cheerful disposition'. She is described also as 'motherly', her ruling interest the loving care of her family. Her relation to Søren was that of many a mother to a youngest son: according to some female cousins he was 'terribly spoilt and naughty' and always hanging around his mother even at age fifteen.[14] Also, while it is true that Kierkegaard repeatedly mentions his father in his authorship, his mother appears indirectly too. His brother Peter Christian tells us that Kierkegaard 'had preserved many of his mother's words in his writings', and at least one happy childhood anecdote involving a mother seems to be directly from his own life.[15] It is also worth mentioning that when his mother died, he was profoundly distressed.[16] Finally, one can add positively to the picture of the mother, two of the facts concerning her that are usually taken negatively. First, she was a harmonious, loving person, but not intellectual. The men of the family were not only educated, they were highly intellectual, with temperaments permitting personal struggle and conflict. Second, Kierkegaard does not mention his mother plainly in his total author-ship, but his father has a prominent position (in Kierkegaard's journals and in the dedications of the many edifying or religious discourses). Taken positively, we can say that Kierkegaard's mother would never figure in the authorship because his mother was never a source of problem, conflict or strict ethical-religious demand. We can add that she does not figure in the intellectual universe of the men of the family, and that she would therefore never figure in relation to the discourse of the authorship.[17]

Kierkegaard's father, Michael Pedersen Kierkegaard (1756–1838), was one of the nine children of Peder Christensen Kierkegaard and Maren Andersdatter Steengaard.[18] His story is undeniably a dramatic one. The Kierkegaard family were serf-tenant farmers on the small church farm[19] in Sædding, three miles south-east of Ringkøbing in Jutland. Not surprisingly, such a large family existed under conditions of extreme poverty, and Michael left his home in 1777 in order to work as a shepherd boy with a relative in another parish. The life of a shepherd boy was, however, a harsh one,[20] for a lad could find himself alone on the heath exposed to the pangs of hunger and whatever the weather had to offer. Michael, not surprisingly, was one day overwhelmed by the misery of his situation and solemnly cursed God for leaving him in such a situation without help. Shortly after this, his life was to change completely. An uncle in Copenhagen sent to the family in Sædding for an apprentice in his clothing business and Michael left Jutland in the autumn of 1768.[21] In Copenhagen he did so well that at the age of 24 he was an independent businessman. In 1794 he married Kirstine Nielsdatter Røyen, sister of business partner Mads Nielsen Røyen. The marriage was childless, and his wife died two years later of pneumonia. Just before his second marriage to Anne Lund, Michael Kierkegaard gave up his business, a wealthy man. He may have retired because he now had (together with what he probably inherited from his uncle) more than enough, but evidence seems to point to the *fact* of his rise to wealth and his second marriage as at least contributing, if not major, causes. Frederik Sibbern, Professor in Philosophy at Copenhagen University, tells us (1863) that Michael Kierkegaard gave up his business out of a kind of hypochondria, believing he would soon die. If we place the various events of Michael's life thus far together, a possible explanation emerges.

As a boy, Michael was highly religious. This might have been assisted only by the general religious tradition of Bible, Church and catechism, plus the natural seriousness of the West Jutland peasantry; yet one can add to this the factor of Pietist revivalism in

8

the Sædding region in the 1720s and the influence of the Moravian Congregation with a Moravian revival especially in the period 1761–92.[22] Thus we can see probable influence on Michael of Pietist-Moravian revivalism, with thoughts of sin, personal conversion, and Christ emphasized as the man of sorrows. When he was confirmed in Nicolai Church in Copenhagen, 1773, the sermon was preached by a Pietist-Moravian pastor, and Michael joined a Copenhagen parish with Pastor Saxtorph, a Pietist-Moravian, attached to it. So it is not surprising to find Michael Kierkegaard the established businessman attending the Moravian Congregation Meeting House in Stormgade later on.[23]

Given such a background, to curse God for one's situation, even as a lad, would be no light matter. One can imagine Michael's shock when he experienced the sudden call to Copenhagen, the guilt he felt, a guilt he in fact still retained as an old man of 82, since he saw his action as the commission of the unforgivable sin against the Holy Spirit. It would seem that he experienced his growing prosperity as part of a coming righteous punishment in which God gave him all possible material mammon only to take everything else away. When his first wife died childless after two years of marriage, his relation to Anne Lund may therefore well have been the quest for consolation in the face of the beginnings of disaster. Such a relation would be especially serious in the light of the Moravian view of marriage, where the sexual element was demoted to the level of indifference and marriage partners were decided in the Moravian community (as late as 1820) through the casting of lots.[24]

On top of this, it must be remembered that Michael Kierkegaard was highly reflective and intelligent. In his years as an apprentice he must have received a certain amount of good schooling, though he seems largely self-taught, and after retirement from his business he devoted himself to theology, philosophy and aesthetics, possibly because in Copenhagen he experienced for the first time questions posed by the Enlightenment concerning God's existence, the meaning of the world and the foundation of morals. So, everything considered, it is not surprising that he withdrew from business to devote himself to a spiritual rather than a material life, while it is certain he suffered from spiritual melancholia.[25]

Apart from involvement with the Moravian community, Michael Kierkegaard and his family also came for periods in contact with a Norwegian pastor, J. Bull (who seems to have laid weight on the ethical content of Christianity), with the Pietist pastor J. O.

Thisted, and, not least, with Jakob Peter Mynster (1775–1854), a pastor of the cathedral congregation, who came to have enormous significance for both Michael and Søren.[26] In the early 1800s, the Moravian Congregation (anticlerical in tendency) not surprisingly formed a major opposition to the rational Enlightenment Christianity affecting the State Church. Mynster, a brilliant anti-rationalist preacher, attracted those who were not strongly anticlerical, but who opposed rationalism,[27] while his emphasis on the individual's spiritual life, on prayer and meditation and on the State Church as the institution nurturing personal spirituality, would prove attractive to many. Thus the Kierkegaard family came to attend both Mynster's services and meetings at the Moravian Congregation. Mynster had taken his degree in theology at the university in 1794. He spent eight years as a private tutor before taking up his first pastorate at Spjellerup in 1802. It was in 1811 that he began his pastorate with the cathedral congregation. In the following years, among other activities, he lectured in psychology at the Pastoral Seminary, and in 1826 became Royal Chaplain. He became Primate of the Danish Church (Bishop of Zealand) in 1834.

The years 1797–1813 brought Michael and Anne Kierkegaard a large family of seven children (three girls and four boys); but the deaths of all but two of his family, Søren and his elder brother Peter Christian, were to confirm Michael Kierkegaard in his sense of guilt and the wrath of God. If his guilt concerning cursing God had not previously been coupled with the idea of divine retribution at some point, the contrast between increasing material benefits and the many deaths[28] would all too easily lead such a religious temperament to such an interpretation. Certainly the father's brooding temperament seems to have burdened the life of at least Peter Christian and Søren, and much has been written about the effect of the revelation of his father's secret or secrets on Søren, the episode of the 'great earthquake'.[29] Yet it is here that a sense of balance is called for. While it is true that Michael's religious seriousness received a melancholic emphasis from his sense of guilt, and it is also true that he was the authoritative patriarchal figure in the home, it is incorrect to see the home as isolated from society, a totally unhappy place, or the father as a domestic tyrant.

From descriptions left of Michael Kierkegaard we can gather that he was strict and punctilious. Everything had to happen at the correct time and in the correct manner and be done by the appointed person in the household. He expressed his displeasure not in scolding but in the seriousness manifested in his reproaches. He was dignified, precise, careful, and strictly economical in money matters, though occasionally very generous. His niece tells us that his honesty went almost too far in its anxious conscientiousness. He reacted to serious misfortune with a surprising serenity and resignation, but could let himself be upset by small domestic trifles, at which point his underlying brooding nature came to the surface. Despite his strictness, he was not without kindliness towards people (including children) or lacking practical concern for the well-being of those outside the home. Nor is the home to be seen as entirely gloomy. Although the parents were elderly and thus inclined to run the home on old-fashioned lines, the family came into contact with other families, while the marriages of Nicoline, Petrea and later Peter Christian, brought a cheerful element to the life of the family. From correspondence and descriptions of the home we get a picture of Michael and Anne Kierkegaard as honest, upright Christians with friendly goodwill towards acquaintances as well as family, presiding over evenings which included nephews and nieces, and which also included good food and harmless card games. Thus we must see the Kierkegaard family as having a wide range of connections with family and friends, and it is reasonable to assume that the Kierkegaard home resembled the homes of other well-to-do families to a fair extent, despite being clearly old-fashioned, less bourgeois and less worldly.

The problem arises, however, in the contrast between the harmonious life of the home in its character of new gentry, solidly and firmly rooted in religion, and the life of secrets and inner spiritual conflict. This contrast did not seem to reveal itself fully until the family at the fine Nytorv home had been severely reduced in size by death. While we know something about the father's secrets we do not know exactly what Søren Kierkegaard's own problem or problems were, although there are indicators. We know that Michael Kierkegaard brought his children up strictly, where both morals and religion were concerned. Duty and obedience were fundamental to the father, and the children were expected to learn the value of obedience to duty and to accept a strict Christianity. In his spiritual melancholia, Michael Kierkegaard dwelt much on the harsher elements of Christianity: on sin, on the righteous God of the Old Testament, on the sufferings of Christ and the martyrs. A sense of the value of obedience to duty was of course not special to the Kierkegaard home, even if it was emphasized there, for the idea of obedience to specific duties was strongly underlined in Balle's catechism to be found in every home, learned by all children, and used in the schools. There is every reason to believe that the story of Judge William's introduction to duty in Kierkegaard's *Either/Or* comes from Kierkegaard's own life, while we know he had to study the catechism along with his brothers at school.[30] What was unusual in the Kierkegaard home was the strict religious upbringing combined with the father's spiritual melancholia, a melancholia that Kierkegaard felt had been projected onto himself and which, together with the upbringing, had deprived him of the experience of being a child. His father was inwardly a melancholic old man, and he caused Søren to share both this experience and (at least for a time) the belief that all the children would die before the father.[31] Thus, while Kierkegaard received the impression that his father was 'the best father', to be respected and revered, he was also later to perceive that he had been terribly wronged through childhood imposition of Christianity with a strongly negative, world-denying spiritual emphasis. This had made him anxious concerning natural human instincts, yet he came to see he had been made anxious about the naturally human, even though he had suspected that guilt rather than goodness underlay his father's extreme godliness.[32] Given that Søren was never blessed with robust health, as his many descriptions of himself indicate,[33] we can see that both religious environment and heredity point strongly away from a physically active life to an intellectual life and to the life of the spirit. Certainly it prepared the way for his decision to renounce marriage with Regine Olsen in 1841.[34] The renunciation of marriage appears in Kierkegaard's authorship as arising from some family and/or personal secret that could not be revealed in the frank relationship of marriage. It also appears as voluntary renunciation for the sake of God and because of some prior religious commitment. Kierkegaard was already 'in a monastery' in 1843 when he wrote *Either/Or*, his first major work,[35] and it is in the authorship that one can mark the main tensions of Kierkegaard's life: a tension between the elements of religiosity and genius in his character, leading to a tension concerning his work in life (pastor or writer), and, finally, a tension in the authorship between world-affirming and world-denying Christianity.[36]

Like his brother Peter Christian, Kierkegaard was educated (1821–30) at Borgerdydskolen (the School of Civic Virtue). In 1830 he went to Copenhagen University. He was supposed to be reading theology, but he read widely in other subjects such as literature, and like many another student, ran up debts that his father had to help him repay. His 'wild life' as a student was hardly very wild by twentieth-century standards. It probably seemed very bad to Kierkegaard because of its contrast with strict Christian ideality. As a person he was very sensitive, highly intellectual and witty and extremely imaginative. As he lets us know in *The Point of View* and other places, he was good at presenting himself in the role of man-about-town in order to hide his inner nature and feelings from the world. Criticisms of Kierkegaard for living the luxurious life of a wealthy person also need to be considered carefully in the light of his personal conflict concerning giving up the world for the life of a poor rural pastor, in the light of his insistence that he is an author and in no way representative of proper Christianity, and in the light of the bourgeois attitude to wealth at the time – the view that if one had wealth one used it.[37] When his father died in 1838, however, he settled down to finishing his degree with thoughts of following the intended career of pastor.[38] In 1840 he entered the Pastoral Seminary and became engaged to Regine, but the following year saw the breaking of the engagement. After his doctoral dissertation *On the Concept of Irony* in 1841, he settled down to the life of an author, remaining all his life in Denmark except for some short trips abroad.[39] While one can perceive great tensions in his authorship, his life on the surface was a quiet one except when he engaged with the satirical paper *The Corsair* in the 1840s,[40] and later, when he openly attacked the Danish Church for its failure to state what true Christianity in his view really was. It was during this attack that he died in November 1855, only 42 years of age.[41]

If one looks at the question of Michael Kierkegaard's religiosity from the viewpoint of tension between Moravian Pietism and State Church Mynsterianism, one can also see it as a tension in the family between rural and urban religion, between peasant pietism and the Golden Age religiosity of bourgeois city life. Søren was to resolve the tension by emphasizing the validity of personal, world-denying religiosity. Peter Christian resolved it by becoming a Grundtvigian.[42] Since 1536 Lutheran Christianity had been the official State religion of Denmark. Despite a certain amount of official, though limited, toleration granted to small groups such as Jews, Calvinists and Roman Catholics, in the period of absolute monarchy (1660–1849) Danish citizenship was restricted to baptized and confirmed members of the Lutheran State Church. In

this period the State Church was simply part of the royal adminis-
tration, and being an evangelical Lutheran was part of being a
Dane. While the government allowed reasonable latitude to the
clergy, lay movements and individual religious initiatives were
frowned upon.[43] It is thus not surprising that in the dominant
Danish Golden Age ideology a continuity was seen between the
visible and invisible kingdom of God, with the spiritual realm
firmly related to earthly prosperity.[44] The clash between pietistic
and rationalistic religion must therefore be seen in the context of
the Danish understanding of the synthesis between the religious
and political worlds.

In eighteenth-century Enlightenment Christianity, the emphasis
was on God, immortality and good works;[45] Jesus Christ was moral
example to be followed and Christianity was expected to be
compatible with reason. The rationalist Danish theology of the
early part of the nineteenth century can be seen as represented by
Henrik Georg Clausen (1759–1840), but it was his son, Professor
of Theology Henrik Nicolaj Clausen (1793–1872), who became the
object of an attack by Nikolai F. S. Grundtvig (1783–1872) when
in a treatise on Catholicism and Protestantism, Clausen emphasized 'the principle of Scripture' as the basis of Protestantism and
insisted on the necessity of the rational interpretation of Scripture.
Clausen introduced modern historical-critical Bible exegesis into
Denmark, and he saw professors of biblical theology as the experts
in explaining Scripture. For Grundtvig, such an emphasis on elite
specialists, and especially Clausen's emphasis on Scripture at the
expense of the community of the Church, was intolerable.[46]

Grundtvig came from a family of pastors.[47] Following in the
family footsteps, he took a degree in theology at Copenhagen
University in 1803. He underwent a period of spiritual crisis in
1810–11, but went on to become pastor at Præstø in 1821 and, in
1822, pastor at the Church of Our Saviour in Copenhagen. After
the libel case provoked by his attack on Clausen, his writings
were censored (until 1837), and he was without a pastorate until he
became pastor of Vartov in Copenhagen in 1839. Although
Grundtvig could not deny the need for Bible exegesis, he saw also
a need for some brief definition of Christianity for the benefit of
Christians unskilled in theology. The result of his deliberations was
his 'matchless' or 'unparalleled' discovery: the distinction between
the spoken 'living word' in the sacraments and creed, and the
written word. The Christian community gathered round the sacraments in the confession of Christ, an unbroken chain of baptized

individuals in community, became for Grundtvig a kind of apostolic succession bound to the sacraments instead of ministry. The heart of the Grundtvigian view can thus be seen to be an existential experience of God in Christ as the living Word, proclaimed at baptism and communion and heard in the Church from the beginning, a living word in which Christ as the Word is present as he is in the sacraments.[48] It was to Grundtvigianism that Peter Christian turned, whereas Søren was to remain critical of its historico-ecclesiastical assumptions.[49]

Mynster and Grundtvig can thus be seen as two types of reaction against the prevailing Enlightenment religion of the late eighteenth and early nineteenth centuries.[50] We find both reactions present in the Kierkegaard home, for Mynster came to have great influence on Michael Kierkegaard, and Peter Christian left the Moravian Congregation to become one of Grundtvig's earliest supporters. Both Mynster and Grundtvig paid visits to the Kierkegaard residence; Peter Christian brought home leading Grundtvigians who were drawn into intellectual debate also with Michael Kierkegaard, a debate to which young Søren was surely an attentive listener if not participant.

Finally, something needs to be said about the influence of philosophy on Danish Christianity as it relates to Kierkegaard's background.[51] Like his father and elder brother, Søren was gifted at philosophical and theological discussion, a talent that he exercised on, among others, one of his tutors at the university, Hans Lassen Martensen (1808–84). Martensen came from Schlesvig and had spent his childhood in Flensborg. In 1817 the family moved to Copenhagen, where he won a scholarship to the Metropolitan School. In 1832 he took an excellent theology degree at the university, completing his education with a study tour in Germany (1834–36). Martensen became lecturer in Theology with Moral Philosophy at Copenhagen University in 1838 and Professor of Theology in 1840. In 1845 he became Royal Chaplain, later succeeding Mynster as Primate of the Danish Church in 1854.[52] Martensen, because of his background, was naturally interested in German intellectual life and found himself particularly attracted by Schleiermacher (1768–1834) and Hegel (1770–1831), also by Franz Baader (1765–1841). This led him in the direction of mysticism as well as philosophy, and to a conception of existence as a series of Hegelian contrasts. It was a conception of existence firmly centred on religion and ideas about God, however, and the basic idea filling all his writings was that of the possibility of uniting faith and thought in the creation of an all-comprehensive synthesis in which all oppositions could be reconciled. All knowledge was to be united harmoniously, with Christianity as the central point, and Hegel's philosophy became his tool in the construction of Christian dogma, the construction of a speculative theology that could mediate between rationalism and orthodoxy. It thus appears to have been Martensen rather than Heiberg who made Hegelianism the ruling philosophy in Denmark for a time,[53] but as Kierkegaard saw, Martensen never seriously engaged himself with the question of whether such a reconciliation was really possible,[54] and Kierkegaard's own philosophical thinking is directed against the prevailing Danish Hegelianism, which, in his view, directed attention away from the individual's ethical-religious existence to a mistaken preoccupation with intellectual speculation concerning the objective world.

Kierkegaard, despite his respect for Hegel's greatness, objects against Hegelianism as he encountered it that it confuses thought and existence. He sees it as a descriptive picture (with a heavily historical bias) of how things are in the world. God is included pantheistically in the system of existence, with Christianity treated as a stage in the ongoing world-historical process in which philosophy is a higher, superior stage. He objects that it is assumed that this vast system is morally good in its outworking, its final result, but since the system is logically necessary and includes both bad and good in its historical progress, the individual's moral decision must be illusory, a consequence not assisted by the further thought that also in the system the individual is subordinate to family and family to the idea of the State. Kierkegaard also dislikes the Hegelian use of Descartes' method of doubt, since he sees that doubt can develop into a thoroughgoing scepticism that undermines everything. Briefly summed up, one can say that Kierkegaard's idea of truth is different from the Hegelian. For Hegel, truth is primarily the entire system of existence, for Kierkegaard, truth has primarily to do with the individual, with how one lives. It is in this spirit that one must understand Kierkegaard's famous Gilleleie Journal entry of 1835, in which he speaks of the contrast between truth as an individual ethical-religious experience and truth as objective knowledge. In one place in the entry, he says – in words since engraved on a stone at his favourite place on the North Zealand cliff-top – 'What is truth but to live for an idea?'[55]

Notes

1. Books consulted for this chapter, concerning Kierkegaard's family background and youth, are: Villads Ammundsen, *Søren Kierkegaards Ungdom* (Copenhagen: Universitetsbogtrykkeriet, 1912); Sejer Kühle, *Søren Kierkegaard: Barndom og Ungdom* (Copenhagen: Aschenhoug Dansk Forlag, 1950); Grethe Kjær, *Den Gådefulde Familie* (Copenhagen: C. A. Reitzels Boghandel, 1981); Grethe Kjær, *Barndommens ulykkelige Elsker* (Copenhagen: C. A. Reitzels Forlag, 1986); Grethe Kjær, *Søren Kierkegaards seks optegnelser om den Store Jordrystelse* (Copenhagen: C. A. Reitzels Forlag, 1983); Steen Johansen, *Erindringer om Søren Kierkegaard* (Copenhagen: C. A. Reitzels Boghandel, 1980); T. H. Croxall, *Glimpses and Impressions of Kierkegaard* (London: James Nisbet & Co. Ltd., 1959); Henriette Lund, *Erindringer fra Hjemmet* (Copenhagen: Gyldendalske Boghandel Nordisk Forlag, 1909); Walter Lowrie, *Kierkegaard* (London: Oxford University Press, 1938); Walter Lowrie, *A Short Life of Kierkegaard* (London: Humphrey Milford/Oxford University Press, 1944); Johannes Hohlenberg, *Sören Kierkegaard* (New York: Pantheon Books Inc., 1954; Octagon Books, 1978); Ronald Grimsley, *Kierkegaard* (London: Studio Vista, 1973); Peter Rohde, *Søren Kierkegaard* (London: George Allen & Unwin Ltd, 1963); Elmer H. Duncan, *Sören Kierkegaard* (Waco, TX: Word Books, 1976); Carl Koch, *Søren Kierkegaard og Emil Boesen* (Copenhagen: Karl Schønbergs Forlag, 1901).

2. Some outstanding figures that can be mentioned are the sculptor Bertel Thorvaldsen (1770–1844), Hans Christian Ørsted the scientist (1771–1851), Adam Oehlenschläger the poet (1779–1850), Johan Ludvig Heiberg (1791–1860), who was poet, aesthetician, critic, translator, director of the Royal Theatre and the introducer of Hegel's philosophy to Denmark. His wife, actress Johanne Luise Heiberg (1812–90), and his mother, author Thomasine Gyllembourg (1773–1856), must also be mentioned. Another important figure is Hans Christian Andersen (1805–75), best known for his fairy tales, but also the author of a number of books and poems. Finally, there is Nikolai Frederik Severin Grundtvig (1783–1872), mentioned later in the chapter.

3. During the Napoleonic wars (1793–1802; 1803–15), Denmark lost its fleet (1801), was bombarded by the English (Copenhagen, 1807), suffered national bankruptcy (1813) and the loss of Norway the following year. The years 1794 and 1795 had already seen terrible fires in Copenhagen.

4. Kierkegaard's life occurs under three monarchies: Frederik VI (1768–1839 – Frederik was regent for his father Christian VII 1784–1808), Christian VIII (1839–48) and Frederik VII (1848–63). Reasons for the political stability can be seen in the character of the Danish people and the character of Frederik VI, whose period of rule saw important reforms. He also took a personal interest in the welfare of his people and, despite some political short-sightedness, endeared himself to his subjects. Thus his fear of revolution spreading from France in 1789 to Denmark was unfounded. One can finally see

grounds for stability in the fact of a small-scale manageable monarchy where unity was implied in a Protestant Lutheran monarch in charge of a Protestant-Lutheran nation, the religious and political spheres forming a whole. See EPW, pp. vii–xxxvi.

5. For example, Walter Lowrie, *Kierkegaard*, p. 24, contrasts with the 'prodigious impression' made by Michael Pedersen Kierkegaard on Søren a picture of his mother as one who 'counted for little in the household'. Lowrie goes on to tell us that Kierkegaard never mentions his mother in the authorship, and that the fact that 'he had no mother he could adore' is surely the reason why he was unable to marry. 'He associated no noble and tender thoughts with woman as mother.' Patrick Gardiner, *Kierkegaard* (Oxford: Oxford University Press, 1988), p. 3, tells us that Kierkegaard's mother 'was illiterate' and 'appears to have played a somewhat shadowy part' in Kierkegaard's upbringing. These descriptions fail to do justice to Kierkegaard's mother.

6. This may account for the fact that Kierkegaard in his authorship in addressing 'the individual' especially mentions 'the common' or 'ordinary' person.

7. For a period Søren Jensen seems to have supplemented the care of his few livestock with work as parish clerk and schoolteacher. Søren Jensen was married to Maren Larsdatter. They had six children, two sons and four daughters.

8. Anne Lund was first in service in the home of a Jutland hosier, Janus Pallesen Thorning, a neighbour to the Røyen family. She was confirmed in Jutland in 1786.

9. Rohde, *Søren Kierkegaard*, pp. 34–5, suggests that Anne can hardly have been 'any great attraction' to Michael Kierkegaard, but it is interesting to compare the widower's epitaphs for the two wives: Kirstine Kierkegaard, aged 38, 'is buried under this stone which her surviving husband has dedicated to her memory'. Anne Kierkegaard, aged 67, has 'gone home to the Lord . . . loved and missed by her surviving children and friends, but especially by her old husband'.

10. See, e.g., Lowrie, *Kierkegaard*, pp. 24–5, and Duncan, *Sören Kierkegaard*, pp. 18–19.

11. Croxall, *Glimpses*, fn. 5, p. 51.

12. Koch, *Kierkegaard og Boesen*, pp. 11–12, tells us that Councillor Boesen, a friend of the family, pleaded for the girls on several occasions concerning their use as servants. The girls were also expected to take care of their brothers' domestic needs.

13. Lund, *Erindringer*, pp. 19–20; Croxall, *Glimpses*, p. 51. She is also briefly mentioned by her first employer in Jutland as 'honest, faithful and hard-working': Kühle, *Kierkegaard*, p. 13.

14. Ammundsen, *Kierkegaards Ungdom*, p. 44, cf. fn. 2, p. 23, suggests that Kierkegaard's closeness to his mother as a teenager was probably because it was easier to get his own way by appealing to her, whereas his father was strict and unbending.

15. Croxall, *Glimpses*, pp. 91–2; FS-JY, fn. 1, p. 194; SV, XII, p. 454 (FSE/JY). Another example of a possible indirect allusion to Kierkegaard's mother may well be in SV, VIII, p. 101 (TA), where he

18

refers to the woman who carried an unrecognizable one under her heart.

16. Hans Lassen Martensen, *Af mit Levnet* I–III (Copenhagen: Gyldendalske Boghandel Nordisk Forlag, 1882–83), I, pp. 78–9; EPW, fn. 37, pp. xvi–xvii. Martensen's mother tells us that she 'had never in her life seen a person in such great distress as S. Kierkegaard was over his mother's death'.

17. Interestingly enough, the distinction Kierkegaard makes in his authorship between the natural character and tasks of men and women may be in part inspired by his experience of life at home. He sees woman as closer to nature than man. She is unreflective, and the harmonious, stable centre of the home, filling it with values arising out of a spontaneous religiosity. He sees man as reflective, having spiritual struggles. His tasks are outside the home.

18. There were five sons and four daughters. Maren Steengaard's brother, Niels Andersen Seding, is said to have been the first person to leave Sædding to settle in Copenhagen, and is the uncle who made it possible for Michael Pedersen Kierkegaard to go to Copenhagen.

19. The family name Kirkegaard, later changed to Kierkegaard, comes from the Danish *kirke* = church and *gaard* = farm.

20. Both Michael Kierkegaard and his cousin were to create foundations in Sædding to help supply money for the teaching of children and for the sick and poor. His son, the Bishop of Aalborg, Peter Christian, also gave similar financial support.

21. H. P. Barfod, *Til Minde om Biskop Peter Christian Kierkegaard* (Copenhagen: Karl Schønbergs Forlag, 1888), pp. 13–15; PAP, VII, 1 A 5 (JP). Michael was chosen to go possibly not only because of any personal wish, but also because he was still under the age when (until 1788) serfdom bound people to their place of residence. In the 1780s and 1790s he lived in Copenhagen at Købmagergade 82, now 43.

22. The Danish Moravians or Herrnhut community originated from the branch of the Moravian Church in German Saxony. On Danish Herrnhutism and its emotional anti-intellectual character and gradual decline, see Bruce Kirmmse, *Kierkegaard in Golden Age Denmark* (Indiana: Indiana University Press, 1990), pp. 31–5.

23. Koch, *Kierkegaard og Boesen*, pp. 10–11.

24. PAP, X, 1 A 310 (JP).

25. Michael Kierkegaard paid particular attention to the philosophy of Christian Wolff (d. 1754) then seen both as a threat to Christianity and as a possible intellectual foundation against atheistic tendencies coming from French and English thought. I use the term 'spiritual melancholia' rather than 'depression' in order to avoid connotations of clinical depression, even though in Michael Kierkegaard's case his condition at the turn of the century seems to have been linked to sickness of some kind (Kühle, *Kierkegaard*, p. 15). Søren Kierkegaard, when he speaks of his own and his father's condition, uses the word 'Tungsind', literally 'heavy-mindedness', and not 'Depression'.

26. Another figure with whom Michael Kierkegaard came in contact was Pastor Jens Hornsyld, who seems in his writings to have devoted much attention to major Old Testament figures such as Abraham and David.

27. Kirmmse, *Golden Age Denmark*, pp. 34–5. On Mynster generally, see pp. 100–35.
28. Apart from prosperity arising from doing good business and inheriting wealth from his uncle, Michael Kierkegaard had also preserved his property during the fires of Copenhagen (1794, 1795), and during the bombardment of Copenhagen in the Napoleonic war (1807). He became even more prosperous after the national bankruptcy of 1813 through having had his money invested securely. Of the daughters, Maren died at 25 of some mysterious illness, Nicoline and Petrea died at 33 of childbirth. Of the boys, Søren Michael died at 12½ of a playground accident and Niels Andreas at 24 in America of an illness. Kierkegaard's mother died of an illness in 1834, and in 1837, Peter Christian's first wife Elise Boisen died.
29. PAP, II A 805 (JP). Much has been written about the nature of the family secrets. Kjær, *Store Jordrystelse*, is especially recommended concerning the father's secret. On Kierkegaard's secrets, see, for one possibility, Leif Bork Hansen, *Søren Kierkegaards Hemmelighed og eksistensdialektik* (Copenhagen: C. A. Reitzels Forlag, 1994).
30. Nikolai Edinger Balle, *Lærebog i den Evangelisk-christelige Religion indrettet til Brug i de danske Skoler* (Copenhagen: in many editions, starting 1791). Balle's catechism replaced Erik Pontoppidan's *Sandhed til Gudfrygtighed* (Stavanger: in several editions, starting 1737), and became a best-seller. Balle was Primate of the Danish Church in the period 1783–1808. He was anti-rationalist. The catechism is concise and well-written, and while it is theologically conservative, it follows fashion in containing teaching (a large section) on virtues and duties. SV, II, pp. 239–40, 242 (EOII); Kirmmse, *Golden Age Denmark*, p. 37. See also Chapter 5.
31. According to Kierkegaard, Peter Christian seems also to have been affected rather negatively by the father's strict religion, at least for a time. PAP IX A 411 (JP).
32. PAP, VIII,1 A 177, 680, 663; IX A 71, 411; X,2 A 454 (JP).
33. PAP, VIII,1 A 177, 577; XI,1 A 268, 277; IX A 74 (JP).
34. Regine Olsen (1823–1904), daughter of Councillor Terkild Olsen and Regine Frederikke Malling.
35. SV, XIII, p. 526 (PVMA, p. 18).
36. See Watkin, 'Journals and Works', esp. pp. 46–9.
37. See EPW, pp. xiii–xvi.
38. Peter Christian Kierkegaard (1805–88) like Søren was educated at Borgerdydskolen and at Copenhagen University. He studied also in Berlin, Göttingen and Paris (1828–30) and became pastor at Pedersborg near Sorø. He was Bishop of Aalborg 1857–75, and for a while in later life Minister of Culture and Church Affairs. He retired early from his bishopric because he, too, became afflicted by some form of deep spiritual melancholia. See Otto Holmgaard, *Peter Christian Kierkegaard* (Copenhagen: Rosenkilde og Bagger, 1953); Carl Weltzer, *Peter og Søren Kierkegaard* (Copenhagen: G. E. C. Gads Forlag, 1936).
39. Apart from a short trip to Sweden in the summer of 1835, Kierkegaard's travels overseas were limited to four study tours to Berlin in 1841, 1843, 1845 and 1846.

40. See COR.
41. He appears to have died of some virus infection with tubercular complications. Niels Thulstrup (ed.), *Breve og Aktstykker vedrørende Søren Kierkegaard* I–II (Copenhagen: Munskgaard, 1953–54), Document XX (LD, p. 28).
42. It has been suggested that the 'three revivalists' from Kierkegaard's play *The Battle between the Old and the New Soap Cellars*, PAP, II B 13, p. 293 (EPW, p. 112, note 39, p. 264), are meant to be Peter Christian with two (at that point) staunch fellow Grundtvigians: Jacob Christian Lindberg (1797–1857) and Andreas Gottlob Rudelbach (1792–1862).
43. Membership of the State Church, with few exceptions, was thus compulsory and Church ceremonies had civic consequences. Baptism, confirmation, and marriage celebrated by the Church were compulsory. The baptism of the children of Baptists at one period took place with the help of the police. Peter Christian Kierkegaard, when he became pastor, declined to assist at forced baptisms. Confirmation was (and still is) part of the process of coming-of-age. See P. G. Lindhardt, *Grundtvig: An Introduction* (London: SPCK, 1951), pp. 82–3; Kirmmse, *Golden Age Denmark*, pp. 43, 130.
44. Kirmmse, *Golden Age Denmark*, pp. 27–8, 74, 133–4.
45. 'Gud, Dyd, og Udødelighed' – God, Virtue and Immortality, the slogan epitomizing the Danish Enlightenment.
46. H. N. Clausen, *Catholicismens og Protestantismens Kirkeforfatning, Lære og Ritus* (Copenhagen: Andreas Seidelin, 1825). Grundtvig attacked Clausen in *Kirkens Gienmæle* (Copenhagen: 1825): Kirmmse, *Golden Age Denmark*, pp. 35–6, 211–12.
47. His father was pastor in Udby.
48. Grundtvig was to achieve international fame for his genius as pastor, poet, historian, hymnwriter and politician. He is also known as an inspiration behind the Danish Folk High School movement. On Grundtvig see: Lindhardt, *Grundtvig*; Niels Lyhne Jensen (ed.), *A Grundtvig Anthology* (Denmark and Cambridge: Centrum/James Clarke & Co., 1984); Kirmmse, *Golden Age Denmark*, pp. 199–237.
49. E.g. PAP, I A 60–62 (JP); SV, VII, pp. 12–43 (CUP).
50. On the influence of romanticism see Kirmmse, *Golden Age Denmark*; Kjeld Holm, Malthe Jacobsen and Bjarne Troelsen (eds), *Søren Kierkegaard og Romantikerne* (Copenhagen: Berlingske Forlag, 1974); Svend Erik Stybe, *Universitet og Åndsliv i 500 År* (Copenhagen: G. E. C. Gad, 1979), pp. 112–35; Svend Erik Stybe, *Copenhagen University 500 Years of Science and Scholarship* (Copenhagen: The Royal Danish Ministry of Foreign Affairs, 1979), pp. 128–62.
51. It is not possible here to go into the question of the various philosophical influences on Kierkegaard. Gardiner, *Kierkegaard*, pp. 15–31, provides a helpful introductory chapter on the philosophical background. Also helpful are relevant sections of: Alastair Hannay, *Kierkegaard* (London: Routledge & Kegan Paul, 1982) and Gregor Malantschuk, *Kierkegaard's Thought* (Princeton, NJ: Princeton University Press, 1971); Niels Thulstrup, *Kierkegaards Forhold til Hegel* (Copenhagen: Gyldendal, 1967); Niels Thulstrup, *Kierkegaard's*

Relation to Hegel (Princeton, NJ: Princeton University Press, 1980). See also general Kierkegaard bibliographies for works on specific philosophers. Kierkegaard's philosophy teachers at the university were Professor Frederik C. Sibbern (1785–1872) and Poul Martin Møller (1794–1838), Professor of Philosophy at the University of Christiania (Oslo) 1826–30 and at Copenhagen University 1830–38. Poul Møller was Kierkegaard's favourite teacher, good friend, and great influence on his life: EPW, fn. 26, p. xiv.

52. On Martensen, see Kirmmse, *Golden Age Denmark*, pp. 169–97.

53. Johan Ludvig Heiberg introduced Hegelianism into Denmark in the 1830s. Heiberg's main philosophical declaration or programme is to be found in his *Om Philosophiens Betydning for den Nuværende Tid* (Copenhagen, 1833). See Kirmmse, *Golden Age Denmark*, pp. 136–68; Rohde, *Kierkegaard*, pp. 28–30. Carl Henrik Koch, however, in his *En Flue på Hegels Udødelige Næse* (Copenhagen: C. A. Reitzels Forlag, 1990), argues that Kierkegaard must have seen Adolph Adler as standing for the Hegelianism that gripped young theologians in about the year 1840. Kierkegaard in the 1840s was to spend much time on his analysis of Adolph Adler's personal religious 'revelation', concluding that Adler's previous intense involvement with Hegel's philosophy was partly to blame. On Martensen and Hegel, see Kirmmse, *Golden Age Denmark*, pp. 169–71, and Reidar Thomte, *Kierkegaard's Philosophy of Religion* (Princeton, NJ: Princeton University Press, 1948; Greenwood reprint 1969), p. 6.

54. In his *Christian Dogmatics* (Edinburgh: T. & T. Clark, 1871), Martensen eliminates all the difficulties confronting reason, although in the final chapter a stumbling block seems to appear in the doctrine of eternal damnation. In his *Christian Ethics* (Edinburgh: T. & T. Clark, 1881–82), Martensen attempts to achieve a synthesis of humanism and Christianity; but rather than a Hegelian synthesis, it seems to be more a surrender of Christianity to humanism. See Thomte, *Kierkegaard's Philosophy of Religion*, pp. 6–15. See Law, *Kierkegaard as Negative Theologian*, pp. 35–50, for an excellent concise presentation of Kierkegaard's criticism of Hegelianism.

55. PAP, I A 75, fn. p. 55 (JP): 'Hvad er Sandhed andet end en Leven for en Idee?'

3

Existence and vocation

THE WORLD AND OUR PLACE IN IT

Although, as we shall see, Kierkegaard heavily distanced himself from his writings through pseudonyms, it is essential for a clear understanding of his aims and authorship to grasp the nature of the idea for which he himself lived. I will thus sketch out the outlines of his own world-view, put together on the basis of a thorough examination of all his writings. It is not possible here to give the necessary detailed arguments to demonstrate that what is presented is in fact Kierkegaard's world-view. I will, however, mention one weighty consideration that is much overlooked, namely, that the structure of the argumentation in his writings reflects his personal commitment to a Christian world-view. Despite his respectful treatment of other positions, Kierkegaard's personal belief, that the Christian world-view is the factually correct one, appears in how he presents other views. An example of this is his discussion of the Greek's relation to fate as a world-view, where he argues that fate can be the object of anxiety but has no independent existence in itself. Kierkegaard's pseudonym, Vigilius Haufniensis, is not undertaking a Christian psychological investigation like Anti-Climacus in *The Sickness unto Death*, yet his underlying assumption is the actual existence of the Christian God.[1] As we shall see, the pseudonymous understanding of the structure of the human psyche is also developed on the basis of a Christian world-view. In what follows, I thus make no apology for referring to aspects of Kierkegaard's own view expressed through his pseudonymous writings, where I find such references to be adequately supported by material under his own name about his authorship, by personal journal material (as opposed to other material in his papers), and by the criterion of consistency of the personal perspective that emerges.

Kierkegaard's Christian universe is dualistic in the sense that he sees the entire realm of existence as divided into the temporal world, time, and the eternal world, eternity. Temporality consists of space–time as we experience it in the succession of moments making up the days and years of our lives.[2] Eternity is the everlasting realm of God, transcending temporality.

Kierkegaard avoids scientific or philosophical descriptions of the relationship between time and eternity, firstly, because he thinks that an element of faith is unavoidable in one's commitment to the objective factuality of one's world-view. Secondly, he objects to the mistaken idea that objective historical 'facts' can be securely proved and are superior to a person's faith-commitment. Thirdly, he dislikes a preoccupation with immortality and eternal life as a person's final personal destination. This encourages a person to act for the sake of eternal reward, through fear of eternal punishment, or to develop a casual and superstitious belief in Christian doctrines concerning immortality and the resurrection.[3] However, Kierkegaard believes that one's final personal destiny is factually decided in this life by how one lives in relation to divine grace. Although he speaks of hell, there is no dualism between God and a devil. God permits suffering and evil and is in total control of creation. Hell in Kierkegaard's thought is not a separate realm in relation to heaven and earth but a state of being, as can be seen from Kierkegaard's *The Sickness unto Death*, where the one who has not lived rightly comes to experience after death an eternity of the hell of isolated personal despair that that individual developed while living.[4]

It can be seen that there are two approaches to the question of world-view; the intellectual approach to the intellectual content of the view, and the question of how one should exist or live in relation to it. It is Kierkegaard's emphasis on this second question that has led many to class him as an *existentialist*. Where the intellectual commitment to the Christian world-view is concerned, this must be through faith, not certainty, and in relation to the objective truth element of Christianity there are two levels of faith-commitment. With respect to the intellectual perspective, the one who has faith in a world-view that includes a God or divine being behind everything persists in a continuity of intellectual commitment to the factual validity of what is objectively uncertain, since one cannot prove God's existence the way one can prove a theorem. The only certainty is thus provided by the believer in continuing in the faith-commitment. For the one committed to a specifically Christian world-view, there is also a further level of faith or belief, namely 'against the understanding', since the believer is required to face the 'offence' of Christianity, namely the conflict between the assertion that God is said to be eternal and unchangeable and the assertion that God was born and died as a human being, the lowly historical figure of Jesus of Nazareth. The eternal and unchangeable is thus declared to have undergone change. Here we have objective uncertainty surrounding the facts of the life of an historical person, also in relation to the idea that there is a God, and this is coupled with what appears to be contradictory to reason and expectation.[5] The intellectual tension is described in terms of the contrast between the person's persistence in commitment to the world-view, both intellectually and as a way of life, and the increasing difficulty of the objective content, the uncertainty, to which is added the conflicting element or 'paradox'.[6]

The question of how one should live in relation to Christianity comes to provide an extra element of difficulty, however, because of the growing importance of the figure of Jesus in the Christian world-view as unfolded by Kierkegaard in his authorship. Initially, in *Either/Or*, the demand made on the one espousing a Christian world-view is mild. The individual is expected to live morally, making a commitment to a mild altruism or putting of others first. The task is relatively easy and it seems as if anyone could do this. It is a life-style that could belong to many religious perspectives, and the figure of Jesus is emphasized as the pattern of moral goodness. Yet Kierkegaard explores through his authorship two main kinds of personal development: one in which the individual undergoes a spiritual development within the life-style, and another in which the individual's intellectual understanding of the life-style undergoes development. Especially in his *Concluding Unscientific Postscript*, Kierkegaard depicts the individual striving to actualize a higher level of moral life within a religious context, still within a social context, but firmly centred on a personal relation to God and with a certain amount of detachment from the world.[7] However (and here Kierkegaard underlines what he sees to be the specific difference between Christianity and similar types of religious life-styles), the individual may develop to make the dismaying psychological discovery that the maximum of effort to be and do good coincides with the maximum discovery of guilt and sin in the self. The psychological discovery is made that in relation to what Christianity demands as the ideal, one is a sinner.[8] The discovery may also arise more suddenly through an understanding of what Christianity really calls for. This may occur through, for example, an intellectual movement to Christianity from a world-view with a relatively undemanding moral code, or through a movement from a milder perception of Christianity to a perception of its radical demand.[9] The individual is unable to reach the standard set up in the Christian life-style, and the figure of Jesus now becomes important as the redeeming Christ who both reveals the nature of God's goodness and yet makes good the deficiencies of the sinner. The factor of the individual's moral and religious development both psychologically and intellectually is the explanation of what appears at first sight to be a contradiction in Kierkegaard's authorship in his discussion of ethics and religion. The ethical is the highest sphere of infinite requirement and the only link between God and a person; it is a sphere through which the individual passes, yet one in which the individual remains.[10]

Although Kierkegaard discusses other world-views in his authorship, particularly those of the Greek world and Judaism, and finds those containing eternally valid moral norms acceptable,[11] his own belief-commitment is, as we have seen, to the objective accuracy of the Christian world-view. What he comes to stress in his authorship, though, is the accuracy of his interpretation of Christianity as a life-style that, if taken seriously, makes a radical demand on the individual. The total altruism of Christ in giving his life for sinners is the pattern of total self-denial for the individual to follow. Christianity in this light ceases to be a mild altruism in a social context and appears as the demand to forsake everything, including one's family, to follow Christ, take up one's cross and suffer the hatred of the world.[12]

The difference between the two realms – of temporality and eternity – is therefore increasingly stressed as Kierkegaard in his authorship moves further into his description of Christian ideality as total altruism. In the light of eternity seen as the kingdom of undying self-sacrificing love, temporality, even at its best, is an egoistic realm. Danish Lutheran Protestantism is seen as the 'spiritless secularism' of a 'rejoicing in life' totally lacking the presupposition for the Lutheran use of the Pauline 'justification by faith through grace', namely Luther's 'troubled conscience' and the ascetic-monastic background. In other words, there can be no resort to the divine forgiveness of sin through Christ without some effort and an admission of what Christian ideality is.[13]

Thus Kierkegaard's Christian world-view calls for the individual to strive to live an altruistically good Christian life, not in order to achieve a place in heaven, but as a thankful response to the sacrificial life and death of Jesus. Only after one has admitted what Christian ideality is and made a serious effort to live the Christian life dare one have recourse to Christ in his role of Saviour. There can be no divine grace without first facing the demand of the divine law.[14]

Since we are placed by God in the realm of temporality and, on the Christian view, have potentiality for eternal life, our relationship to the realm of the eternal is in two directions. There is a backward-looking direction to the life of Jesus as the eternal God entering time at a past historical moment, even though this becomes, for the believer, a present experience starting from the moment of his or her faith-commitment to Christ in the present. There is also a forward direction for the individual to eternity, not only because eternity after death (whether heaven or hell) lies ahead of the believer, but also, and especially, because the individual has eternal life now only as potentiality or possibility. The individual can embark on the development of his or her spiritual or eternal self in the present, and, by continuing in the ethical-religious life of faith, actualize that potentiality as far as it is possible for a sinful human being in this life.

Kierkegaard's view of our place in the world and of our relation to the eternal realm thus turns out to be very concrete where the question of life-style (as opposed to belief in doctrines or ideas) is concerned. His description of the self and its place in the world comes to us in terms of the psychology of the development of the self, and since it is psychology, it also considers the self's development in the context of other world-views. Kierkegaard's investigation presupposes, however, the basic validity of the Christian outlook with respect to the nature of the factual structure of the self and its relation (or misrelation) to the realm of eternity. Kierkegaard investigates the psychology of the self not merely on the basis of his own presuppositions about the world, but also from his observation of other people in his environment and of other cultures he read about. He presents his findings chiefly in two of his works, *The Concept of Anxiety* and *The Sickness unto Death*.

In *The Concept of Anxiety* (1844), Kierkegaard explores the nature of the human self as it develops to the state of self-conscious behaviour. The individual emerges either from egocentric unreflectiveness in childhood, or at any age, to awareness concerning the possibility of action or particular actions. God has created each human being with the possibility of free action and with the potentiality of freely relating to God.[15] Thus a person is seen as born into the world as human self with the potentiality of becoming an authentic individual self in a relationship to the eternal – ideally to the eternal Christian God, but minimally to some other concept of the eternal. As Kierkegaard makes clear throughout his authorship,[16] the self that arrives in the world has capacities of knowing or thinking (both imaginatively and logically), of willing and feeling, and can be said to be a *synthesis*, or combination, of body and psyche.[17] The individual is also equipped with the potentiality for spiritual and eternal life, and it is to the extent that an individual chooses to actualize this possibility that there ought to, and can, arise a second synthesis, one between the temporal and the eternal, the finite and infinite, necessity and freedom. By 'necessity' Kierkegaard does not mean 'predestination', but simply historical factors over which a person has no control, namely heredity and initial environment. The second synthesis between the individual's freedom and necessity occurs through the exercise of moral choice, and it is through the development of self-awareness and consciousness that the individual develops his or her spiritual or eternal nature, 'transparent' in the sense of having come to know the self and reaching beyond the self to and in the God-relationship.[18]

In *The Sickness unto Death* (1849), Kierkegaard from a Christian perspective describes the further psychological state of despair that arises through the various forms of misrelationship a human can have to the eternal. In all cases of misrelationship, the individual fails to develop a proper relationship to the eternal God. Again Kierkegaard uses 'synthesis' language, but here the emphasis is on the need for the individual rightly to develop the second synthesis between the temporal and the eternal. Both in *The Sickness unto Death* and in other works,[19] Kierkegaard speaks of the self or 'ideal self' which is outside and inside the self, and is the idea of the self that the individual should seek to actualize. The idea is inside a person, because within the imagination; but outside, in that it is drawn from an ideal of moral and/or religious personhood derived from the culture. Finally, linked to Kierkegaard's view of living spiritual or eternal life now, in a futureward direction, is his notion of 'repetition'. Repetition is continuity of moral life in relation to God and also, of course, in relation to one's fellow human beings. One persists in, or 'repeats' such moral activity day by day, doing one's best as far as one is able.[20]

Kierkegaard's concept of the human self can thus be described as relational. Each person needs to find and do his or her task in life, but each person must also have the self as moral or ethical task[21] in that each one has a responsibility to live according to the ethical-religious idea, and, in Kierkegaard's own view, this is found ideally in Christianity, in which the individual, by doing the truth, lives for the idea.

KIERKEGAARD'S VOCATION – MONASTERY IN THE WORLD

As we saw earlier, Kierkegaard from the 1848 standpoint of *The Point of View for My Work as An Author* (1859) saw himself 'in a monastery' when he wrote *Either/Or*. From this work, and from some journal entries, it is clear that it was particularly the broken engagement to Regine Olsen that lay at the start of his authorship proper and gave it its impetus. For Kierkegaard, the experience of breaking with Regine, getting her to break off the engagement, was so overwhelming that he felt that after this there could be a choice only between a life of total worldliness or 'the cloister'. Since he saw himself as already decided for the monastery, this sense of choosing one thing or the other indicated to him how impossible it was to be religious only up to a point. Choice of the monastery, however, was not for a Danish Protestant the joining of a religious order, but initially a strict regime of spiritual reading while he wrote *Either/Or* (under the pseudonym 'Victor Eremita') and then other works. For a time he still thought he might overcome the problems that prevented his marriage, but Regine married Johan Frederik 'Fritz' Schlegel, and Kierkegaard seems to have seen himself as 'pre-pledged [to God] early in childhood', a statement that might merely refer to his strict religious upbringing or could imply some more conscious form of commitment that ideally must preclude marriage.[22]

Kierkegaard tells us that after writing *Either/Or* he intended to devote himself to the life of a pastor in the country (where conditions would have been hard), but his book was a success, and this distracted his attention from ordination as a country parson. Yet the idea of the pastorate returned, and Kierkegaard tells us that with 'every new book I thought: Now you must stop'. He came to think that religious and religiously inspired authorship was permissible to him for a period, but always in the background he saw 'Governance', as Kierkegaard calls God, ready to send him off to the country parsonage. He still continued to live his life under 'strict religious rules', but saw himself as a penitent, not in any way saintly. While writing *Either/Or* he even went as far as to let Copenhageners think of him as an idler amusing himself at the theatre. When he was not writing he enjoyed walks in the city (where he knew and talked to stallholders and the poorer classes) and tours in the countryside.[23] With the publication of *Concluding Unscientific Postscript* on 27 February 1846, Kierkegaard thought that he now had definitely finished writing, and this work indicates a summing up and conclusion of what has gone before.[24]

It was at this point, however, that Kierkegaard felt called upon to engage with *The Corsair*, a powerful, widely circulated paper[25] that dealt in anonymous political satire. The paper's original aim was to serve the cause of political liberalism, but it speedily degenerated into a publication that indulged in exploiting facts, rumours and gossip to destroy the personal reputations of its victims. For a variety of reasons Kierkegaard felt he should take a stand against it and did so in an article published in the paper *Fædrelandet* on 27 December 1845. He immediately became yet another victim of *The Corsair*'s satirical pen in a series of attacks on his person carried on at a trivial level and lasting many months. *The Corsair* presented Kierkegaard in the character of a crazy idiot, and this resulted in his becoming a figure of fun on the Copenhagen streets. It also gave him a new insight into what it was to be an author, since being one in such a difficult environment involved more asceticism than living the life of a rural pastor.[26]

By 1848 yet another event occurred to strengthen Kierkegaard in seeing writing as his vocation. In March 1848, Denmark underwent a peaceful revolution that led to the change to a constitutional monarchy in 1849. At the Reformation, the Church had been absorbed into the State establishment without thought of establishing it in any way as a separate entity or of giving it its own constitution. Thus, as we have seen, Church and State formed one entity under an absolute Protestant Lutheran monarch. Not until the eighteenth and nineteenth centuries was the Church specifically identified as 'the State Church'. The new constitution said that 'the constitution of the People's Church will be ordered by law', but as Bruce Kirmmse points out,[27] statements made about the Church in the new constitution were vague. Since a Church constitution would either have to be in the hands of a clerical elite or else come under the democratic direction of a lay majority, it was found preferable to understand the new constitution as meaning that the Church would be regulated by laws on a case-by-case basis. This in fact put control of the Church in the hands of the new political Assembly. Bishop Mynster accepted that the teachers of the Church could be appointed by those governing the State if these were also members of the Church. A godly State would forward the task of the Church, while the task of the Church was to permeate and transform the State. Mynster shared the Golden Age view that the kingdom of God was linked to temporal well-being and prosperity. Christianity for Mynster thus set the seal of approval on a God-fearing tempo-rality, and since one's participation in the official Christianity of the Establishment was tied up with one's citizenship of Denmark, the one wishing to remain outside the established Church was, in Mynster's eyes 'a foreigner'. So Mynster accepted the results of the constitutional change in 1849 because he saw this change as retaining the old idea of 'Christendom' under the name of 'People's Church' instead of 'State Church'.[28]

In a journal entry from 1849, Kierkegaard says that his previous praise of Mynster is valid only if the concepts 'state church' and 'established Christendom' are valid concepts. If they are not, then 'Bishop Mynster can be attacked'. Kierkegaard, between 1838 and 1848, had lived on the sum he inherited from his father. By 1849 his financial situation had deteriorated to the extent that he thought seriously about getting a post, either as rural pastor or in the Pastoral Seminary. However, in this period he also considered the need of 'stepping forth in character', that is, putting ideals into practice whatever the cost – which might be that he caused offence that made it impossible for him to get an official appointment.[29]

Kierkegaard tells us in his journals of 1853 that he had always believed that he would never have to earn his living, partly because he would die young (Kierkegaard's poor health would reinforce this idea) and partly because God would have mercy and not thus add to his personal cross in life. He also speaks of a persistent thought over the years that he might be among those destined to be sacrificed in some way for others. He says that the New Testa-ment teaches that 'to be loved by God and to love is to suffer', though it is presumptuous to pray for personal suffering as if one were one of the 'glorious ones' chosen by God. He asks whether love by God or for God can possibly be combined with enjoying life. He also says that like his contemporaries he had at one stage thought this was possible, but his own experience and his understanding of the New Testament point to suffering in the world for those seriously committed to a relationship with God. The question Kierkegaard particularly raises at this point is: 'does the New Testament recognize any other kind of Christian than "the disciple"?' For Kierkegaard the answer is in the negative, and the picture of Christianity as a suffering renunciation points Kierkegaard strongly away from Bishop Mynster's view of it. Mynster, in his opinion, has subscribed to the idea that all within the official Danish Church are Christians – a Christian is one who 'accepts the doctrines, rests in grace, but does not in the more rigorous sense enter into "imitation"'. Mynster has 'abolished, completely omitted' the imitation of Christ in the rigorous sense of imitation, as if nothing is wrong. He 'substitutes . . . the most tasteful worldly culture for Christian heterogeneity with this world, a rare, uniquely refined enjoyment of this world and this life for renunciation and self-denial'.[30]

Given his deepening emphasis on Christianity as the imitation of Christ, it is not surprising that Kierkegaard reflects a great deal about his own life, work and God-relationship. He asks himself whether being a writer is not a 'splendid distraction', whether he could continue writing if he found work and thus financial security. He sees that to disregard security could be a kind of spiritual arrogance. Yet to starve seems more likely to be Christianity, since 'Christianity is not a sum-total of doctrinal propositions but is service in character'. He also lets us understand that he has tried practising asceticism for half a year but has given it up because it seems 'sophistical'. On the other hand he has scruples about the thought of daring to 'profit temporally by proclaiming – Christianity, which is renunciation of things temporal'. He solves the tension initially by leaving everything to God in an obedient readiness to do God's will in a cheerful trust in God's love, though this does not mean that he is free of the tension of the struggle to work out what that will is.[31]

In 1849 Kierkegaard had still been considering the possibility of winding up the authorship and getting a position. At the same time he realized that the trend of his writing pointed to a clash with the established 'Christendom'. His thoughts about the work of a modern pastor grew more negative, thus clearly making it difficult for him to reconcile this with applying for a pastorate or even the work of teaching pastors. It also became increasingly clear that if the Establishment found his writings offensive, it would definitely not wish to employ him. Thus in 1851, although he again saw his authorship as finished, he tells us he has given up the idea of seeking an appointment. By 1852 he is even more negative about pastors, and in 1854 he was to thank God for not letting him become a pastor 'in the sense in which one is a pastor around here these days, which is a mockery of Christianity'.[32]

Kierkegaard thus moved towards a collision course with Mynster, even though as late as 1851 he still admired him and found that the bishop's sermons told him 'exceptionally well what to do'. Mynster appeared to him as doctrinally correct, a powerful preacher, but also confusing and deceptive in that he somewhat 'altered Christianity'. Mynster was an orthodox Lutheran and an enemy of rationalism, but his religion was an ethical religiousness with Christ as the divine teacher assuring us of God's grace and providence and of the truth of the natural religion of the Enlightenment.[33] For Mynster the individual's correct attitude to God was one of resignation and submission to his will, the following of conscience and the doing of one's duty.[34] Kierkegaard had been 'brought up' on Mynster's sermons, but he also found he was educated and developed through his own unfolding authorship.[35]

In a note written in 1852, Kierkegaard briefly reports his movement from 'enjoyment of life with an admixture of the ethical' to 'enjoyment of life with an ethical-religious admixture', finally looking towards 'suffering, renunciation, the religious – to become less than nothing in this world'. Presumably he found he could accept Mynster's preaching (given that it retained all the Christian doctrinal elements) as long as he found he could stay with 'enjoyment of life with an ethical-religious admixture', but not when he considered seriously the gospel injunction to give up everything for Christ, finding that 'outside of the N.T. there is no official definition of what Christianity is'. Unlike Grundtvig in his condemnation of official Danish Christian religiosity, Kierkegaard did not ask why the Lord's word had disappeared from God's house, but rather why power had departed from the proclamation of God's word.[36]

One may ask here why Kierkegaard so easily accepts the New Testament as sole authority, given his emphasis on faith and the uncertainty of the historical. The answer is to be found firstly in the fact that through his pseudonym Climacus, he criticizes both biblical authority and church authority where these are appealed to as validating the certainty of religious claims and eliminating the need for faith. Seen from that perspective, Grundtvig's 'matchless discovery' of an oral tradition that preceded and validated Scripture was unacceptable. Secondly, the authority of the Lutheran Church was Bible-based, and therefore one would be able to compare the life-style the State Church commended as being in accordance with the Scriptures with the actual Scriptures that Church appealed to. Finally, Kierkegaard rejects church authority as soon as it becomes worldly and attempts to control people temporally with the help of Christianity, whether this means the authority of the Vatican or the authority of a State Church.[37] Thus his rejection of the Pope is on a par with his rejection of the Protestant bishop, yet 'Catholicism and Protestantism' are, in Kierkegaard's view:

> actually related to one another as a building which cannot stand is related to buttresses which cannot stand alone, but the entire structure is able to stand, even very stable and secure, when the building and the buttresses together give it stability. . . . In other words, is not Protestantism (or the Lutheran principle) really a corrective, and has not a great confusion been brought about by making this normative in Protestantism?[38]

What is called for is true preaching of the Christian way of life. Excess emphasis on works coupled with the sale of indulgences in Kierkegaard's view received its corrective in Luther's action and Luther's emphasis on grace. But Lutheranism taken as a norm leads again to 'Christendom' in which, a nice, 'grunting, prosperous bourgeois, provided that he is generous to the pastor is supposed to be the earnest Christian'.[39]

For Kierkegaard, an important difference between Catholicism and Protestantism is that Catholicism had the monastic life, asceticism and fasting, in the background, whereas in Protestantism these had become regarded as ridiculous, foolish and unreasonable.[40] In journal entries from his last years Kierkegaard criticizes Protestantism for treating monasticism as a flight from the world and for slipping into 'profane worldliness'. There thus needs to be a retreat back to the monastery. The fault with monasticism was not 'asceticism, celibacy, etc.'. The fault was that the demands of Christianity were reduced, in that the monastery was allowed to regard itself as containing extraordinary Christians – while the sheer nonsense of the world was treated as ordinary Christianity. But 'asceticism and everything belonging to it is merely a beginning. . . '. Monasticism should appear as 'hidden inwardness' (hidden personal religiosity) in the world, though the danger of the latter is that the 'hiddenness' may be a sign of its not being there at all.[41]

The task that crystallizes itself out for Kierkegaard in his last years is thus nothing less than a new reformation through the re-introduction of Christianity into 'Christendom'. This is to be done, not by bringing down the established order or reforming Church or doctrine, but through a dispersal of the illusion that Christendom is Christianity, through an emphasis on Christian ideality that acts as a corrective upon the Establishment. Throughout Kierkegaard sees himself in terms of writer, penitent, secret agent, spy, instrument, corrective; one gifted with the extraordinary, that is, a genius, but not 'the extraordinary', that is, not an apostle or one chosen by God in some kind of direct encounter. Kierkegaard's God-relationship is 'through reflection', not immediate experience. He is 'without authority', not even ordained, and while his task is new, he brings nothing new in terms of special revelations from God. He is not a witness to the truth or martyr-figure.[42]

In all his life the nearest Kierkegaard came in the direction of immediate nonreflective religious experience of a more mystical nature was in 1838 when he spoke of an 'indescribable joy'. In 1848 he described his broken engagement as leading to 'a religious awakening', and in the same year he had an experience of his whole nature 'being changed'. Again in the same year he spoke of 'an overwhelming perspective on his life' when he was aware of the guidance of Governance in being granted the extraordinary.[43] These latter experiences seem, however, to be of a more psycho-logical and intellectual nature although part of his personal God-relationship. Where his personal relationship to the Church was concerned, he was a regular churchgoer and communicant, also preaching in church, even as late as 1851.[44] Thus Kierkegaard never in any way saw or presented himself as a special religious figure or as a dissident sectarian, and he took great pains to make sure he could not be made the unwitting founder of any sectarian group.

In the 1850s Kierkegaard did his best to avoid coming into collision with Mynster and the Establishment, hoping that his writings would inspire the bishop to fresh insights through an understanding of what Kierkegaard was trying to do. Kierkegaard tells us he did not wish to attack Mynster. 'A little admission from his side', he says, that the religiosity preached by the established Church was not the 'authentic conception of Christianity' would have been enough. We also learn that Mynster was offended by Kierkegaard's publication of *Works of Love* in 1847, and of *Christian Discourses* in 1848; *Practice in Christianity*, published on 27 September 1850, 'distressed him painfully'.[45] In all these works Kierkegaard stressed the Christian life as one of testing, self-denial and suffering. Where Mynster had preached reassuringly about the Christian hope of immortality, Kierkegaard's discourse on 'The resurrection of the dead . . . ' describes immortality as resurrection to judgement.[46] Since Mynster also treated suffering and sacrifice in the early Church as only a necessary stage in the history of Christianity, it is not surprising that Mynster was displeased with Kierkegaard's emphasis on them as necessary for Christians at all times, and with his emphasis on the 'Church militant'. In several journal entries we learn from Kierkegaard that Mynster regarded Kierkegaard's position as 'pitched too high', an odd 'exaggeration' of Christianity. Kierkegaard tells us that Mynster had 'a certain amount of goodwill' towards him, but that he regarded him as 'a suspicious and even dangerous person'. He also disliked Kierkegaard's hell-fire scare tactics.[47]

When Mynster read *Practice in Christianity* he is reported to have said that it was playing 'a profane game with holy things'. To Kierkegaard he said he did not think it would 'prove useful', and characterized it as an attack partly on the theology professor Hans Lassen Martensen and partly on himself. Kierkegaard's polemic against the honorary 'Church triumphant' and pastors making 'observations' from the pulpit seemed to be particularly directed against Mynster, while Martensen would have seen himself in the picture of the philosopher taking offence at Jesus.[48]

In 1853 Kierkegaard looks back to the 1850 publication of *Practice in Christianity*, seeing it as saying 'the specific something I have to say'. It expresses his Christian position or 'thesis' that 'Christianity does not exist at all', is a mirage in which in an appeal to 'objective doctrine and *objectively*, pastors and churches, attention is diverted from what is crucial, the subjective, that we are not Christians'.[49]

Neither Martensen nor Mynster were prepared to accept that there was need for the reintroduction of Christianity into Christendom. Yet of particular importance in the book is Kierkegaard's statement that:

> I have never asserted that every Christian is a martyr, or that no one was a true Christian who did not become a martyr, even

though I think that every true Christian should – and here I include myself – in order to be a true Christian, make a humble admission that he has been let off far more easily than true Christians in the strictest sense [so that] the Christian order of rank may not be confused and the no. 1 place completely disappear as place no. 2 takes over its position.[50]

The significance of *Practice in Christianity* lay particularly in its double role. On the one hand it could be taken as an attack on the Establishment, but it could also be 'a corrective defense' when taken together with the preface and a small section called 'The Moral'. In the preface to the book, Kierkegaard says the requirement for being a Christian 'is forced up by the pseudonymous author to a supreme ideality', but 'the requirement' should be presented, heard, and admitted. In 'The Moral', Kierkegaard emphasizes the need for the individual to face up to the demand of Christian ideality and then continue Christianly in a happy daily life, for, '[i]f anything more' is required, God will let that person know. Further, Kierkegaard makes it crystal clear that he expected Mynster to read the book and react publicly, either by expressing agreement with *Practice in Christianity* or by condemning the work. As Kierkegaard makes clear in *The Point of View*, *Practice in Christianity* became an attack or defence of established Christianity depending on how it was read and judged. If one agreed with the book's call for an admission as to the nature of Christian ideality, it became a defence; if one condemned the book as an exaggeration of Christianity, it became an attack. When the second edition of *Practice in Christianity* was published in 1855, Kierkegaard made no changes to it, but it had been the final test of the established Church, and he notes in that year that had he first then published the book, he would have published it under his own name and he would have removed 'The Moral', thus making it a definite attack on the Establishment.[51]

Kierkegaard tells us that if Mynster had (publicly) maintained that his own preaching of Christianity was genuine New Testament Christianity (thus condemning *Practice in Christianity*), he would immediately have begun his attack on Mynster and the Church. Given Mynster's silence, he waited. He appears to have begun preparation for his attack in the May of 1851, but he continued waiting until Mynster died (30 January 1854) before intensifying his preparation and opening the attack in the paper *Fædrelandet* on 18 December that year. He also tells us that he felt it important to wait in case Mynster did at any point come out with such a public statement about Christian ideality.[52]

The occasion for the opening of the attack (which appears chiefly in 21 articles in *Fædrelandet* and in Kierkegaard's own paper from 1855 *Øieblikket* [The Instant]) was Professor Martensen's funeral eulogy for Mynster, declaring the late bishop to be a Christian 'witness to the truth'. Except for one reply to Kierkegaard at the beginning, Martensen (who was appointed to the bishopric on 15 April 1854) kept silent during the attack which covers the period from 18 December 1854 to Kierkegaard's collapse in October 1855. Kierkegaard's initial article is headed: 'Was Bishop Mynster a witness to the truth?'. Martensen's one reply in the paper *Berlingske Tidende*, 28 December 1854, takes issue with Kierkegaard's definition of such a witness. Martensen suggests that Kierkegaard wrongly defines all such witnesses as martyrs (something Kierkegaard denied). He defends Mynster's status as a witness to the truth and also his Christian teaching, which, he says, contains 'dying to the world' even if not in Kierkegaard's style. In reply, Kierkegaard makes clear that the point is that Mynster could not be such a witness, because far from suffering and self-denial Mynster was an official, a member of the nobility, and a worldly careerist. Mynster was: 'worldly-wise, to a high degree, weak and eager for life's enjoyments and great only as an orator', and he omitted 'the decisively Christian'.[53]

Kierkegaard's attack widens out to include all the clergy on the grounds that there is an incompatibility between being a paid State official in a comfortable living, preaching an equally comfortable Christianity, and what the Christian demand is in the New Testament. He declares 'Protestantism, Christianly considered', to be 'an untruth, a piece of dishonesty, which falsifies the teaching, the world-view, the life-view of Christianity'. Yet Kierkegaard did not see the answer was to become a Catholic, insofar as both Protestantism and Catholicism had become confused through the ecclesiastical notion of the concept 'Church' and 'Christendom'.[54] Although (apart from Mynster, Martensen and a few other clerics) Kierkegaard's attack is directed only generally against pastors, his polemic is savage. For example, *What Christ's Judgement Is About Official Christianity* (1855) starts:

It might seem strange that not till now do I come out with this; for Christ's judgement after all is surely decisive, inopportune as it must seem to the clerical gang of swindlers who have taken forcible possession of the firm 'Jesus Christ' and done a flourishing business under the name of Christianity.[55]

Neither is Kierkegaard averse to using analogical parables offensively as in the story '*First* the kingdom of God', where theological graduate Ludvig Pious (*From*), who can preach a glowing sermon on seeking first God's kingdom, is shown as seeking everything else but that – a career, a well-paid job, and so on. The piece ends by telling people that they have one sin the less on their conscience if they stay away from the current church worship. Finally, one can imagine the anger of the clergy at a comparison of the Church with a dishonourable type of theatre, or on reading that: 'The priests are cannibals, and that in the most odious way.'[56]

On 15 October 1855, when he had almost entirely run out of money, Kierkegaard's health gave way. He was taken to Frederik's Hospital, Copenhagen, where he died on 11 November. Right to the end he expressed no regrets about the intensity of the attack, refusing to tone it down in any way. While some saw Kierkegaard's final writings as a symptom of sickness and insanity, there were also many, as Peter Christian Kierkegaard pointed out in Kierkegaard's funeral sermon on 18 November, who owed to him 'a Christian awakening, or a further development in their appropriation of Christianity'. Although Peter's outlook was so different to that of his brother, it should be noted that he published Kierkegaard's *Point of View for My Work as an Author* in 1859, and he was also responsible for the publication of Kierkegaard's papers.[57]

In his translation, *Kierkegaard's Attack Upon Christendom*, Walter Lowrie says that 'The Moral' and the preface of *Practice in Christianity* 'suggest plainly enough . . . the Catholic distinction between the universal precepts of Christ and the "counsels of perfection"'.[58] The 'evangelical counsels' of poverty, obedience and chastity are not seen as 'necessary to salvation' but are a rule of perfection, instruments of perfection for those who find they have a vocation to follow them. If we look at Kierkegaard's emphasis on ideality from this perspective, then Kierkegaard towards the end underlines these counsels as something one should see as necessary to salvation *before* turning to justification by grace through faith, which thus seems to add up to the Catholic distinction, if serious personal acknowledgement of ideality and some attempt at striving is in fact what is essential to salvation. Yet the matter is more complicated than this. Clearly Kierkegaard,

Mynster and Martensen appreciated the authentic Christianity of the lives of early-Church apostles and martyrs. The important questions arise when one delves more deeply into the question of the nature of Christian ideality.

Firstly, we need to put a question to Kierkegaard concerning his attack on Mynster for failure to live and preach New Testament Christianity. Is he attacking Mynster for living according to the universal precepts of Christ and for preaching these as if they were on the same level of spiritual ideality as the 'evangelical counsels'? That is, is he in the light of the Protestant emphasis on 'justification by faith' denying the distinction between counsels and precepts by asserting that the precepts are counsels? One might then see a contrast between Kierkegaard's denial of a difference between the two in seeing the counsels ideally applying to all, and Mynster's denial of a difference in the direction of emphasis on the universal precepts only, for all those in the post-early-Church period.

It would appear, however, from many texts, that Kierkegaard is attacking Mynster for being a worldly pleasure-seeker parading as a godly man. Even allowing for the deliberately exaggerated language of Kierkegaard's polemical style, we seem to be looking at two different charges and not one. One might, of course, argue that Kierkegaard thought he had been deceived in Mynster, finally discovering from experience that Mynster was merely a worldly careerist. Or one might argue that the concept of the worldly-wise pleasure-seeking careerist (especially when this is a contrast developed in the light of the highest Christian ideality) simply indicates an ordinary prudent pursuit of wealth and happiness and personal interests on Mynster's part, a pursuit that has to be condemned when Christian perfection is in question. Yet however one regards Kierkegaard's view of Mynster's personal situation, the charge of worldliness and pleasure-seeking would seem to be in a different category from the following of Christ's universal precepts. One can imagine many pastors and bishops earnestly seeking to preach and live by the universal precepts of Christ, who would condemn worldly pleasure-seeking and selfish careerism.

This consideration leads to a second question, namely, do two clearly marked levels of requirement (outside the persecution situation of the early Church) come from the New Testament; one, where a person is called upon to strive to follow Christ's precepts in the world; another, where one is exhorted to adopt the evangelical counsels or some extremely self-denying and/or ascetic course of life?[59] To this is linked the question of how far *any* striving is *necessary* to one's eternal salvation through Christ (justification by faith), and secondly, if one feels moved vocationally to follow the counsels of perfection, what does this entail – life as an active religious in the world, or life as, for example, a contemplative away from the world in a strict monastic order?

There is also a further question to be considered, and that is the nature of the psychological–spiritual dimension of existence. Is there a particular way of life that is intrinsically necessary to the development of personal spirituality? Finally, if there is a specific path to be followed – one that would apply in all authentic religions and would be what made them authentic – are religious trials and extra tribulations (as opposed to voluntary self-denial/ asceticism) inevitably part of the package? During the attack on the Church Establishment Kierkegaard may have failed to make clear the distinction between an ungodly worldliness and life according to Christ's universal precepts (in the light of life according to the counsels of perfection), but through his authorship he strives to clarify many questions from the inside, including the psychological perspective. He explores the nature of both levels of Christian requirement, the question of what is intrinsically necessary to spiritual development and some of the trials and tribulations of the spiritual path. If Kierkegaard fails to be sufficiently explicit sometimes during the attack on the Church, one cannot fail to be excited and challenged by his authorship. Did he, however, feel he would succeed in getting his message across to his contemporaries? To answer this question we need to examine his authorship.

Notes

1. SV, IV, pp. 366–7 (CA).
2. On time and eternity and other concepts in Kierkegaard, there are special articles by Gregor Malantschuk in JP. Also see Gregor Malantschuk, *Nøglebegreber.*
3. SV, VII, pp. 11–43, 373–4 (CUP); SV, VIII, pp. 144–64 (UDVS); PAP, XI,1 A 547, 325, 463, 260 (JP). Kierkegaard's own clear references are therefore few and tend to occur in the context of some other theme, e.g. PAP, VIII,1 A 487; X,6 B 232; VII,2 B 235, pp. 143–5 (JP, OAR, pp. 111-12). See Malantschuk, *Kierkegaard's Way*, pp. 79–96. George E. and George B. Arbaugh, *Kierkegaard's Authorship* (London: George Allen and Unwin, 1968), pp. 278–9, point out that Kierkegaard disliked the emphasis placed on immortality in a complacent Platonic direction, instead of on resurrection and judgement. Kierkegaard, however, avoids detailed doctrinal discussion of life after death and Christianity,

while Balle's catechism contains both immortality and eternal life in connection with the idea of a double judgement – at one's death and on the final Judgement Day.

4. SV, VII, pp. 74–6 (CUP); PAP, VI A 62; XI,1 A, 2, 399; XI,2 A 395, 132, 130; VII,1 A 181 (JP); SV, XI, p. 141 (SD).

5. James 1:17–21, SV, XIV, pp. 277–94 (FS-JY); 1 Cor 1:23, PAP, IV C 1, p. 363 (JP). See also Chapter 6 in the section on 'The tension of dying to the world'.

6. Kierkegaard explores these themes particularly in SV, VII, see esp. pp. 171–2, 175, 493–4 (CUP) and SV, XII (PC). His polemic against the academic and clerical intelligentsia attempts to recreate the 'offence' of 1 Cor 1:23.

7. On Kierkegaard's 'Religiousness A', see SV, VII, pp. 335–490 (CUP); Thomte, *Kierkegaard's Philosophy*, pp. 55–96.

8. SV, VII, pp. 169–70, 174 (CUP).

9. On the psychology of types of ethics see SV, IV, pp. 288–96 (CA).

10. SV, VI, p. 443 (SLW); SV, VII, pp. 122, 111 (CUP).

11. Kierkegaard accepts Socrates' attempt to arrive at, and act in accordance with, eternally valid truths; Judaism is acceptable (despite Old Testament emphasis on eternity expressed in temporal continuity of the nation) because its moral law comes from God.

12. Luke 6:22; 14:26–27.

13. PAP XI,2 A 108, 111, 305, 130; XI,1 A 87, 199 (JP); SV, XII, pp. 64–5 (PC); Romans 3:24; 4:16–24; 11:16.

14. Kierkegaard finds it difficult to think that a loving God could let anyone end in hell, even though the notion of universal forgiveness would encourage people in their failure to make an effort. He tries to overcome this difficulty through the thought that the universal conditions for salvation are tailored by God to the individual. PAP, XI,1 A 325, 296, 244; XI,3 B 57 (JP).

15. The Emperor Nero is described as 'a child' because he has never grown up. He has remained in a state of egocentric unreflectiveness; SV, II, pp. 167–70 (EOII). See also PAP, VII,1 A 181 (JP) on God and human freedom.

16. In, e.g., SV, VII, pp. 300 (CUP).

17. SV, IV, pp. 315, 319, 350, 355, 358, 360–1 (CA). The first synthesis is constituted and sustained by spirit, because it is only through reflection and choice, and thus the spiritual side of the self, that the individual can come to develop his or her psycho-physical being. It is important to note here that Kierkegaard (who deliberately re-uses the terminology of the German philosopher Hegel) is not positing a dualism of the self of the kind to be found in the thought of the French philosopher Descartes. Kierkegaard's dualism has to do with the difference between temporality and eternity, which difference bears on his description of the self in its psychical and physical aspects.

18. Through SV, IV (CA) Kierkegaard describes the gradual psychological process of coming to make a choice in the particular instant or moment of time. The possibility of freedom (and hence responsibility for action) creates anxiety in the individual, a gradually awakening state (dreaming, then awakened, spirit) in which the possibility of choice, freedom,

action, ambiguously attracts and repels the individual. The transition to concrete action (good or bad) occurs as a leap.

19. SV, XI, pp. 127–8, 139, 142–3 (SD); SV, II, p. 232 (EOII); SV, XII, pp. 173–6 (PC).
20. Such repetition is different from the false notion of repetition – the pleasure-seeker's attempt to 'eternalize' pleasure, SV, III, pp. 191–209 (FT/R), and from the religious repetition of Christ's incarnation that 'repeats' the eternal in temporality.
21. SV, II, pp. 226, 231 (EOII).
22. SV, XIII, pp. 526, 564–5, 568–71, 578 (PVMA, pp. 18–19, 76–7, 82–7, 97, 162–3); PAP, X,1 A 272, 374; X,5 A 149; IV A 107; II A 347 (JP); Lowrie, *Kierkegaard*, pp. 191–231. Kjær, *Gådefulde Familie*, pp. 29–32, suggests Kierkegaard's father might have exacted some promise from him.
23. SV, XIII, pp. 526, 546–7, 568–71 (PVMA, pp. 19, 48–50, 82–7); PAP, X,5 A 146, pp. 151–2; X,1 A 138, 272; X,2 A 48 (JP). A favourite country tour was Otteveieskrogen or the Nook of the Eight Paths in the Gribskov, a forest in the middle of Zealand.
24. PAP, VII,1 A 4; IX A 54; X,5 A 146 p. 152 (JP); SV, VII, pp. 212–57, [545]–[549] (CUP), 'Glance at a contemporary effort in Danish literature' and 'First and last explanation'.
25. *The Corsair* was started in 1840. It was owned and edited by Meïr Goldschmidt, who edited it (with Peder Ludwig Møller) until 1846. Goldschmidt greatly admired Kierkegaard's pseudonymous works, and Kierkegaard therefore had already had the experience of being praised in *The Corsair* (COR), pp. vii–xxxviii.
26. PAP, X,5 A 146 p. 152; cf. X,1 A 138 (JP).
27. Kirmmse, *Golden Age Denmark*, ch. 7, and pp. 219–20.
28. Kirmmse, *Golden Age Denmark*, pp. 132–5. Kierkegaard was contemptuous that Mynster's idea of protest against the new order came to no more than joining the minority party in Parliament, PAP, X,1 A 385, 541; XI,2 A 399 (JP).
29. PAP, X,1 A 535, 273, 404, 281, 56, 74, 167; X,6 B 60; X,5 A 146, p. 153 (JP); VII,2 B 235, pp. 43–4 (OAR, pp. 36–7).
30. PAP, X,5 A 146, p. 151–3; X,5 A 72, 105; X,3 A 472; X,4 A 296; XI,2 A 283, 437; IX A 41 (JP).
31. PAP, X,5 A 105, 146, 72; X,1 A 156; VII, 1 A 221 229; IX A 54 (JP).
32. PAP, X,2 A 147; IX A 390; X,2 A 157; X,4 A 568; XI,2 A 248 (JP). See Gregor Malantschuk, 'Søren Kierkegaard – poet or pastor?', AN, pp. 3–24.
33. PAP, X,6 B 173, p. 275; X,4 A 511; XI,2 A 312; X,6 B 218, pp. 348–9 (JP); Kirmmse, *Golden Age Denmark*, pp. 100–8.
34. Mynster's sermons from the 1840s show why Kierkegaard found them helpful yet moved away from them. Emphasized is Christian heroism in taking up the cross daily, the duty of being glad in the daily tribulations of life. In a sermon for All Saints' day on continuing the work of the holy ones who have 'brought about the improvement of our Church', the members of the congregation are urged, among other things, to extirpate superstition, work against false piety, strive to keep the good the Church already has and hold fast their faith in the hope of

immortality: Jakob P. Mynster, *Prædikener paa alle Søn- og Hellig-Dage i Aaret* (Copenhagen: Gyldendalske Boghandlings Forlag, 1845), II, pp. 324, 331, 340, 345, 349.

35. PAP, X,6 B 173; IX A 227; X,1 A 273 (JP); SV, XIII, pp. 561–2, 501 (PVMA, pp. 72–3, 151).

36. PAP, X,4 A 663, 56; X,5 A 33; X,3 A 550; XI,2 A 40 (JP); Matt 10:37; Luke 14:26; Kirmmse, *Golden Age Denmark*, p. 202.

37. PAP, XI,2 A 410 (JP).

38. PAP, XI,2 A 305 (JP).

39. PAP, XI,2 A 31; X,5 A 106; XI,1 A 28 (JP). Kierkegaard points out that the corrective should never be made the norm for the next generation.

40. PAP, XI,2 A 305; XI,1 A 263; X,3 A 56 (JP). At Whitsun 1850, Mynster preached a sermon against monasticism.

41. PAP, XI,1 A 134, 198, 263, 443; X,4 A 531, 556 (JP); SV, VII, pp. 411–12 (CUP); SV, XII, pp. 196–9 (PC).

42. PAP, X,2 A 193, 45, 61; X,3 A 565; XI,2 A 21, 36, 346, 250, 150; XI,1 A 136, 460, 268; IX, A 243, 142, 223; X,6 B 232; X,4 A 33, 15, 647, 130; XI,3 B 53, 57; X,1 A 281, 273, 56, 541, 74, 92, 266; VII,1 A 126 (JP); SV, XIII, pp. 543, 559, 563–4, 567–8, 571, 582, 604–5, 501, 505 (PVMA, pp. 43, 68–9, 75, 80–3, 87, 103, 128, 130, 151, 153). For Kierkegaard, religious authority is 'either an apostolic call, or the specific quality of ordination', SV, XI, fn. p. 101 (PA, fn. p. 149; OAR, fn. p. 111). He often calls himself only a *Digter* = 'writer', a word that is often mistakenly in this context translated as 'poet'.

43. SV, XIII, pp. 568–9 (PVMA, pp. 83–4); PAP, II A 228; VIII,1 A 640; X,5 A 146, p. 152 (JP).

44. His edifying discourse 'God's unchangeableness' was given as late as 18 May 1851 in Citadel's Church (Kastellet), Copenhagen. On Kierkegaard and the Church see Howard A. Johnson, 'Kierkegaard and the Church', AC, pp. xix–xxxiii. Howard Johnson (p. xix) says that Kierkegaard ceased attending public worship 'in his last months', but it should be noted that Kierkegaard last attended Holy Communion on 28 May 1852, at the cathedral.

45. PAP, XI,3 B 15, pp. 40–1 (PC, p. 369); PAP, X,4 A 511 (JP). Kierkegaard refers to the Christian ideality of *Works of Love* in *Practice in Christianity*, SV, XII, p. 204 (JP, PC).

46. SV, X, pp. 203–13 (CD, pp. 210–20), cf. note 34 above. Martensen also preached reassuringly about life after death as his Easter Day sermon, 1881, 'Haabets Anker', indicates: Martensen, *Af mit Levnet*, III, pp. 230–42.

47. PAP, X,4 A 474; X,3 A 415, 43; XI,2 A 31; X,4 A 511; VII,1 A 221; XI,3 B 57 (JP).

48. PAP, X,3 A 563; X,4 A 604; X,6 B 226, 137, 113, p. 142; SV, XII, pp. 46–7, 82–3, 115–16, 192–202, 212, 216, 231–2 (PC, also PC, note 112, p. 395). Martensen's *Christian Dogmatics* was published in 1849 and appeared in several editions (2nd impression 1850) and in translation. Kirmmse, *Golden Age Denmark*, pp. 169–97, 175–81.

49. PAP, X,6 B 232 pp. 375, 377–8 (JP).

50. SV, XII, pp. 208, 33–4 (PC).

51. SV, XII, pp. 64–5 (PC); PC, pp. xv, xvii–xviii; PAP, XI,3 B 15; X,3 A
    563, 564 (JP, PC); SV, XIV, pp. 80–1 (AC, pp. 54–5); SV, XIII,
    pp. 507–8 (PVMA, pp. 156–7).
52. PAP, X,6 B 171–236, 194, 226, 232, 225, pp. 359–60; XI,1 A 1; XI,3 B
    216, p. 358 (JP); SV, XIV, pp. 5–10 (AC, pp. 5–9); Lowrie,
    Kierkegaard, p. 517.
53. SV, XIV, pp. 5–30 (AC, pp. 5–22).
54. SV, XIV, pp. 251, 48–9 (AC, pp. 211, 34–5).
55. SV, XIV, pp. 139–49 (AC, pp. 117–24). The body of the attack is built
    on the theme of Christ's condemnation of the scribes and Pharisees,
    Matt 23:29–33; Luke 11:47–48.
56. SV, XIV, pp. 248–51, 235–6, 333–5 (AC, pp. 208–11, 197–8, 268–70).
57. AC, p. 90; Steen Johansen, *Erindringer*, p. 153. Among those who saw
    Kierkegaard as sick were J. H. Paulli, Mynster's son-in-law, Royal
    Chaplain from 1840, and Martensen. Strange to say, by the 1880s,
    Martensen had come to regard Kierkegaard's attack as chiefly one on
    himself rather than on Mynster, but he vaguely saw that Kierkegaard
    might have something to say even though he disagreed deeply with
    him: Martensen, *Af mit Levnet*, III, pp. 12–23. See Croxall, *Glimpses*,
    pp. 105, 127–9, 81–134; Lowrie, *Kierkegaard*, pp. 583–8; Kjær,
    Gådefulde Familie, pp. 40–6.
58. AC, p. xvi; Donald Attwater (ed.), *The Catholic Encyclopædic
    Dictionary* (2nd revised edn; London, Cassell, 1949), p. 179, cf. 126,
    'Counsels' and 'Precepts'.
59. An excellent discussion of this question is to be found in J. A. Ziesler,
    Christian Asceticism (London: SPCK, 1973). Ziesler concludes
    (p. 118) that 'The New Testament, with the one possible exception in
    the Book of Revelation, does not set forth asceticism as the Christian
    path to holiness. Yet something like an *ad hoc* asceticism hangs over
    the head of every committed believer – an asceticism which is based
    not on a concern for personal sanctity, but on readiness to fulfil the
    demands of Christ's call in the task of mission. Like a good soldier, the
    Christian is ready for anything, to have or not to have, to eat or not to
    eat, to marry or not to marry – for a time, or for life. This readiness is
    possible only because he values the good things of this life and enjoys
    them, without being totally absorbed in them.'

4

The authorship

STRUCTURE

Kierkegaard's writings can be divided up into three categories. First there are his journals and papers, containing diary material, drafts of books, notes and letters, and complete or near-complete unpublished writings such as *The Book on Adler*. The second category consists of published works under his own name, including newspaper articles, his dissertation on irony, a review, religious discourses, and a short explanation of the authorship. The third and most difficult category contains Kierkegaard's pseudonymous writings, in which many important issues in human life are discussed, such as the nature of authentic ethics, what it means to believe, the nature and cause of despair. A major link between the second and third categories is the pattern of publication. From the first major work *Either/Or* to *Concluding Unscientific Postscript*, for every pseudonymous work Kierkegaard simultaneously published religious discourse material under his own name. In 1846 *Concluding Unscientific Postscript* (which specifically poses the question of what it means to be a Christian) formed the intended conclusion of pattern and authorship. The work was accompanied this time by a review of a novel (*Two Ages*). The intended conclusion, however, became the literary midpoint of the authorship. From then on, Kierkegaard made the writing of religiously oriented works his major task, and this finally led into his material attacking the Church.

Though seemingly straightforward, the structure of Kierkegaard's authorship is difficult for the reader for several reasons.

One is that it is not always easy to see which parts of the journals and papers are Kierkegaard's private diary as opposed to sketches for a book. There are also fine nuances in the discourse material, which appears under the headings of 'edifying discourses', 'Christian reflections', 'Christian discourses',[1] all of which, however, address the reader's spiritual life in the style of exhortation. Finally, the pseudonymous works are especially difficult because of the many pen-names, the Socratic presentation of the subject-matter, and the application of different disciplines (philosophy, psychology). While some of the works (*Either/Or*; *Stages on Life's Way*) contain a medley of pseudonymous authors, all with different views of life, others (*Philosophical Fragments*; *The Sickness unto Death*) have but one author reappearing in a later work (*Concluding Unscientific Postscript*; *Practice in Christianity*). The subject-matter of the works varies considerably, too. Whereas *Either/Or*, for example, presents the problem of choosing a life-style, *Fear and Trembling* deals with the problem of what grounds could justify Abraham's intended sacrifice of Isaac, while *The Concept of Anxiety* looks at anxiety as a psychological experience. The approach to the various topics presented in the different works is also varied. Some works (*The Concept of Anxiety* and *The Sickness unto Death*) are particularly works of psychology; others (*Philosophical Fragments* and *Concluding Unscientific Postscript*) are philosophical. Others still (*Either/Or*, *Repetition* and *Stages on Life's Way*) are heavily novelistic.

Thus, if one wishes to see what Kierkegaard says about a specific topic, one has to work through discussion presented by the pseudonyms. While a subject occurs again and again, it is treated from different perspectives and outlooks. As a result, the topic is often spread through the authorship. A good example is Kierkegaard's view of the structure of the self, which is dealt with by his pseudonyms. Descriptions of the self occur, for example, in *Either/Or*, *The Concept of Anxiety*, *The Sickness unto Death* and *Practice in Christianity*;[2] but while study of the descriptions gives the reader indirectly an insight into Kierkegaard's own understanding of the self, there is a big difference between Kierkegaard's pseudonymous work and a straightforward treatment of the kind to be found in a book such as Paul Churchland's *Matter and Consciousness*.[3] Whereas in Churchland the question of the structure of the self is abstract, in Kierkegaard the question is connected with concrete human problems. One can go straight to Churchland's book to find his discussion of consciousness, but there is no straight way of

KIERKEGAARD'S AUTHORSHIP

PSEUDONYMOUS WORKS		WORKS UNDER OWN NAME		JOURNALS AND PAPERS	
1834-36	articles by A & B	1836	article	1833–55	JP
1838	*From the Papers of One Still Living*	1841	*The Concept of Irony* (diss.)	1842–43	Johannes Climacus
		1842–51	articles to do with the authorship		
1843	*Either/Or* ed. Victor Eremita (2nd edn 1849)	1843	*Two Edifying Discourses*		
1843	*Fear and Trembling* by Johannes de silentio	1843	*Three Edifying Discourses*		
1843	*Repetition* by Constantin Constantius	1843	*Four Edifying Discourses*		
1843–46	articles to do with the authorship by A. F. ..., Victor Eremita, Frater Taciturnus, A				
1844	*Philosophical Fragments* Johannes Climacus	1844	*Two Edifying Discourses*		
1844	*The Concept of Anxiety* Vigilius Haufniensis	1844	*Three Edifying Discourses*		
1844	*Prefaces* by Nicolaus Notabene	1844	*Four Edifying Discourses*		

Year	Pseudonymous works	Signed works	Year	Other works
1845	*Stages on Life's Way* ed. Hilarius Bookbinder	*Three Discourses on Imagined Occasions*		
1846	*Concluding Unscientific Postscript* by Johannes Climacus	*Two Ages: A Literary Review*	1846–47	*The Book on Adler*
1847		*Edifying Discourses in Different Spirits*		
1847		*Works of Love*		
1848	*The Crisis and a Crisis in the Life of An Actress* by Inter et Inter	*Christian Discourses*	1848	*The Point of View for My Work as an Author* (pub. 1859)
			1848	*Herr Phister as Captain Scipio* (by Procul)
1849	*The Sickness unto Death* by Anti-Climacus	*The Lilies of the Field and The Birds of the Air*		
1849	*Two Minor Ethical-Religious Essays* by H.H.			
1850	*Practice in Christianity* by Anti-Climacus	*An Edifying Discourse*		
1851		*Two Discourses at the Communion on Friday*	1851–52	*Judge for Yourself*
1851		*About My Activity as a Writer*		
1854–55		articles in *The Fatherland*		
1855		*The Instant 1–9*	1855	*The Instant 10*
1855		*What Christ's Judgement Is About Official Christianity*		
1855		*God's Unchangeableness*		

pulling Kierkegaard's view of the self from the contexts in which the discussion is embedded. Despite this, however, one can build up his view from detailed study of his writings, while especially for those new to his thought the outline above may be helpful.

METHOD OF COMMUNICATION

Kierkegaard tells us that he has the Socratic task of revising the definition of Christianity, of destroying the illusion of 'Christendom'. Just as Socrates started from where the people were, so, too, Kierkegaard thinks that the effective religious writer must begin from where the writer's contemporaries are and lead them by use of indirect communication to see truth for themselves.[4] Kierkegaard uses pseudonyms as part of his strategy of indirect communication in order to distance himself from his readers. He sees this as a precaution against the infliction of his private person and views on the reader, who needs space for thought and discovery as he or she responds to the questions put by Kierkegaard through the texts. Another reason is that the very nature of the strategy calls for pseudonymity.[5] Whereas Socrates could involve a number of people in his oral discussion, Kierkegaard is confined to the route of author–text–reader. The various pseudonyms thus form other voices in the community of discussion. One can add to this that Kierkegaard as Climacus in *Concluding Unscientific Postscript* points out that communications concerning a way of existence cannot be direct because one is not dealing with a finished result that is to be directly appropriated and used like a mathematical formula. Existence communications need to be made with Socratic indirectness not only in order to leave room for the individual's free development but also because one cannot directly communicate information to do with personal development. It is an individual matter that concerns an individual unfinished process.[6]

Finally, Kierkegaard saw the use of pseudonyms as a way of making a distinction, not only between himself and the authorship, but between the different viewpoints put forward in the authorship. As Kierkegaard himself put it in the journals: 'As is well known, my authorship has two parts: one pseudonymous and the other signed. The pseudonymous writers are poetized personalities, poetically maintained so that everything they say is in character with their poetized individualities.'[7] Fearing charges of self-contradiction and confused thinking, Kierkegaard in the same passage urges the reader to maintain the distinction between author and pseudonyms and between the various pseudonyms. Failure to do this was one problem that could arise from the use of pseudonyms. Another was the possible failure of the tactic should people read his works and totally miss engagement with the positions presented. It was the possibility of these problems that prompted Kierkegaard to write explanations of his authorship. He finally moved totally into direct communication during his attack on the Church.

The direct religious communication (also used for his published discourses) should not be seen as inconsistent with what Kierkegaard's Climacus says about existence communications. The indirect communication concerns debate about life-styles and their problems, the direct communication has to do with how the Christian life-style exhorts one to live, and assumes a Christian or religiously minded reader. Of the other material under Kierkegaard's own name, his explanation of his writing activity, *About My Activity as a Writer* (1851), and the posthumously published *The Point of View for My Work as an Author*, which he calls 'a direct communication' and 'a report to history', are particularly important when considering his authorship. These works are Kierkegaard's attempt to circumnavigate the risk inherent in indirect communication, namely, that the reader may fail to understand it. From the fact that he wrote them, quite apart from the comments of frustration that occur in his journals about reviews of his works, it can be seen that Kierkegaard clearly saw that his contemporaries might fail to understand his complicated method of communication. Thus the books about his authorship were to serve as an insurance policy against this eventuality.[8]

While the Socratic tactic militates against authorial dogmatism, a reader who has failed to understand Kierkegaard's 'dialectic' or Socratic discussion with the reader misses an essential dimension of the authorship. For example, the reader who embarks on *Either/Or* with the idea that it is a novel of some kind, albeit with some underlying philosophical theme, is likely to share the experience of one of the first reviewers, Johan Ludvig Heiberg, who began reading Part One and vainly sought a vantage point for understanding the work because he failed to grasp that the first volume structurally reflected the personality it was intended to portray.[9] In Part One, the main character is a person whose life lacks substance. Having no particular personal conviction for which to live, beyond natural instinct towards what is beautiful and pleasurable, he follows his changing desires through changing circumstances. Not surprisingly, he experiences frustration and changes of feeling and mood, and this appears as the 'Diapsalmata' or fragmentary aphorisms at the beginning of the work. Thus, the reader needs to see the young man in Part One as a three-dimensional figure, and get into his shoes, so that the disconnectedness of the volume comes together in the unity of a life-style totally lacking real unity. Or, to take another example, one needs to step into the shoes of Johannes de silentio in *Fear and Trembling* and follow him through his inside consideration of the question of ethical conflict in the Bible story of Abraham's intended sacrifice of Isaac, a story too often read easily in the light of the happy ending.

Or, to take one more example, one can follow the path of Johannes Climacus, the nineteenth-century Copenhagener who is concerned with what it means to be a Christian. Here, however, it is not sufficient for many modern readers to be conscious of the Socratic tactic, since there is particularly present a problem absent for Kierkegaard's contemporaries. The nineteenth-century Dane was brought up to accept the Christian heaven or 'eternal happiness' as a real possibility, while an educated Dane would understand the historical and philosophical problems connected with Christianity, especially in relation to the contemporary influence of Hegelian philosophy.[10] A clash between the assumptions of Christianity and Hegelianism is certainly not a central problem today, although many will recognize the problem of the historical justification of Christian claims (that Christ was God, God's Son). In order to grasp the meaning and significance of *Concluding Unscientific Postscript*, apart from reading helpful introductory books,[11] the modern reader can enter into the spirit of the Socratic communication by imagining a different starting position for a modern Climacus, who might ask his questions about religious truth against the background of the findings of modern science.

KIERKEGAARD'S 'STAGES'

Thanks to many of his interpreters, Kierkegaard is probably best known for his description of the stages of human existence. A number of books operate with discussion in the framework of the aesthetic, ethical and religious stages or spheres[12] and are not unreasonable to do so given that Kierkegaard makes his pseudonyms speak of stages. Judge William in *Either/Or* speaks of the aesthetic, the ethical and the religious as 'the three great allies'[13] and Johannes Climacus similarly is made to sum up the entire authorship, particularly describing *Stages on Life's Way* in terms of the three stages while carrying the discussion further using three-stage terminology in *Concluding Unscientific Postscript*.[14] There are, however, two major difficulties with this approach to Kierkegaard's authorship. First, although there is, as we have seen, specific talk of three stages of existence, Kierkegaard both boils them down to two (aesthetic and ethical-religious),[15] and adds to their number like Shakespeare's Falstaff on Gadshill, so that we acquire two stages within the religious (Religiousness A and B) and the transitional stages of irony and humour.[16] In the latter case, the factor of additional stages also gives rise to the problem of how they interrelate.[17]

Kierkegaard uses the terminology of several stages in his author-ship to cover different life-situations. In essence,[18] the aesthete is the one who lives a spontaneous or 'immediate' life and, change-able in feelings, moods and bodily condition, thus interacts with his changing environment. The ethical person lives within the context of choice in relation to moral requirement, not least the moral requirement of that person's social context. The religious person's God-centred life has to do with fulfilment, with the individual's effort and failure to fulfil requirement, and with the actual fulfil-ment seen as coming from God's side through forgiveness and grace. Irony and humour come into the picture as perspectives on life. One can be ironic or humorous in a situation but one can also have irony and humour as standpoints. Kierkegaard presents Socrates as a positive example of irony as standpoint, since through his ironical wise 'ignorance' Socrates endeavours to uncover truth through the elimination of erroneous ideas and prejudice. An amoral pleasure-seeker's perspective can also be ironic, but it is negative in that the irony springs from a fundamental rootlessness and, unrestrained, can come to render everything empty and mean-ingless. Humour is intellectual acceptance of the validity of moral and religious requirement, but it is a reaction to the contrast between requirement and frail human striving. Such a person remains an outsider through staying within the purely intellectual considerations of moral and religious (especially Christian) requirement. Johannes Climacus of *Philosophical Fragments* and *Concluding Unscientific Postscript*, and the pseudonyms Quidam and Frater Taciturnus from *Stages on Life's Way*, represent aspects of the position of the humorist who reacts to life through neither ironic ridicule nor ethical commitment but in painful laughter and legalistic deliberation about the extent of guilt. Related to these perspectives are comedy and tragedy as specific ways of viewing the conflicts and contradictions of existence.[19] The reading of Kierkegaard's authorship thus becomes complicated if one approaches it using the stages as pegs along the way, as anyone who has tried to fit the entire authorship into the stages will soon discover.

The second major difficulty with the approach through the stages is what happens if one stays with the basic three-stage division and tries to apply it to Kierkegaard's authorship. If one looks at *Either/Or*, it is easy to demarcate Part One as the aesthetic stage, but Part Two, despite its easier literary structure (letters and sermon), presents problems. If Part Two is only the ethical stage, what is one to make of the Christian pastor's sermon at the end of the book, which appears to stand for a religious position? Or, if we accept that Judge William's view is ethical, one is left with the problem of the basis and content of his ethics and the thought that one seems somehow compelled to go beyond the ethical to the religious; one must, apparently, drop Judge William and his ethics like the booster stage of a space rocket for a religious position devoid of ethics. This is a contradiction of Judge William's own rejection of a divorce between the ethical and the religious,[20] while the situation is reminiscent of the apparently contradictory position mentioned in Chapter 3 where the ethical is both a transitional sphere or stage and yet the highest one in which one remains, a sphere forming the 'Or' only if taken together with the religious.[21]

To look at Kierkegaard's authorship in terms of objective stages, even when we ignore the consideration that the pseudonyms' views are meant to be different, can thus prove a frustrating exercise that turns what is intended to be three-dimensional into the one-dimensional. At the same time it ignores the situation to which, and in which, Kierkegaard was writing. It is therefore that I will now return to Kierkegaard's thought in its three-dimensional perspective.

Notes

1. See, e.g., the title pages of, SV, III–V (EUD); SV, IX (WL); SV, X (CD).

2. SV, II, pp. 232–3 (EOII); SV, IV, pp. 315, 350, 355, 358 (CA); SV, XI, pp. 127–8 (SD), 173-81 (PC).
3. Paul M. Churchland, *Matter and Consciousness* (Cambridge, MA/ Bradford: The MIT Press, 1993).
4. SV, XIV, pp. 119–20, 352 (AC, pp. 97, 283); PAP, XI,2 A 36, 393 (JP); SV, XIII, pp. 531–3 (PVMA, pp. 25–7).
5. It must be noted, though, that the practice of pseudonymity was common in Kierkegaard's time. On the pseudonyms, see Arbaugh, *Kierkegaard's Authorship*, pp. 40–3, 62–3; Birgit Bertung, Paul Müller and Fritz Norlan (eds), *Kierkegaard Pseudonymitet: Søren Kierkegaard Selskabets Populære Skrifter* XXI (Copenhagen: C. A. Reitzels Forlag, 1993).
6. SV, VII, pp. 55–8 (CUP).
7. PAP, X,6 B 145 (JP); also in EOII, p. 454.
8. It should be noted that Kierkegaard deliberately did not publish the fuller and more personal *Point of View* in his lifetime. See Watkin, 'Journals and Works', pp. 38–41.
9. Watkin, 'Journals and Works', pp. 27–9.
10. E.g. SV, VII, pp. 11–43, 55–103 (CUP).
11. E.g. Gardiner, *Kierkegaard*; and Johannes Sløk, *Kierkegaard's Universe: A New Guide to the Genius* (Copenhagen: The Danish Cultural Institute, 1994).
12. Valter Lindström, *Stadiernas Teologi* (Lund and Copenhagen: Gleerup & Gad, 1943); Malantschuk, *Kierkegaard's Way*; Thomte, *Kierkegaard's Philosophy*, to name but three.
13. SV, II, p. 133 (EOII).
14. SV, VII, pp. 252, 498–500 (CUP).
15. SV, VII, p. 252 (CUP); cf. PAP, VI B 41:10 (JP).
16. SV, VII (CUP, see index references in vol. II).
17. Thomte, *Kierkegaard's Philosophy*, pp. 97–109, contains an excellent discussion of the stages and the problem of their interrelation.
18. As will be shown in Chapter 5 there are variations in the aesthetic lifestyle, and the factor of spontaneity does not mean that aesthetes are unreflective.
19. For example, the situation of a deaf man opening a squeaky door slowly so as to avoid disturbing people can be seen as comic, because he thus makes more noise, and as tragic if his name is Beethoven.
20. SV, II, p. 133 (EOII).
21. SV, VII, pp. 111, 122, 124–5 (CUP).

5

Life in a Christian culture

LIFE WITHOUT CHRISTIANITY

We saw in Chapter 3 how Kierkegaard viewed the psychology of
the development of the human self from lack of consciousness to
self-conscious reflection about the world and choice. Awareness,
especially self-awareness, is important if a person is to develop
genuine maturity of personality. It is not only the child, however,
who needs to develop such an awareness. In his authorship
Kierkegaard indicates two major ways in which an 'adult' can fail
to mature, both of which have in common that the person in question is prisoner of 'necessity' or controlling forces that inhibit the
awareness necessary for the achievement of personal freedom.

Such a one is the *Spidsborger*,[1] or philistine, who is absorbed in
material and commonplace things. Kierkegaard takes up this term
emphasizing the element of absorption and lack of self-awareness.
The *Spidsborger* or philistine, in Kierkegaard's version, can be anyone in society. In worldly terms, that person may even be a highly
successful, well-educated, cultivated citizen, respected by all. The
problem with the *Spidsborger* is total lack of real freedom, even
though he or she lives the illusion of making choices. Although
Kierkegaard is therefore unable to create a pseudonym consciously
presenting that position, philistinism is attacked throughout the
authorship by anyone with a clearly reflected attitude to life.

Johannes the Seducer jeers at the emptiness of his engagement
to Cordelia, at the absence of choice although all the conventions
are present. Johannes Climacus attacks the philistine's attachment
to relativity, Anti-Climacus diagnoses absence of possibility, while

Kierkegaard accuses the philistine of letting cosy living replace ideals. He illustrates this in his example of the cultured but religionless young man who finds himself compelled to go through the motions of being Christian when his baby is baptized, and the tradesman who is a churchgoer in order to secure the confidence and business of his customers.[2] The hypocrisy is not conscious. Each follows the normative etiquette and practice of society and can even, as the tradesman does, give reasons for going along with the crowd. In neither case, though, is the person a Christian. If the ruling creed of the society were dialectical materialism, both men would sign up as Marxists. Social and economic pressures dictate their action, and the person in question fails to realize this, through lacking the individuality supplied by authentic selfhood. The philistine is thus merely a numerical member of the crowd instead of being an individual in a community.[3]

The second major way an 'adult' can fail to mature is through staying with the natural instinct for what is pleasurable and beautiful – with the life of the senses. As we saw earlier, Kierkegaard's understanding of the human psyche is that one is born into the world with the possibility of becoming a self. Initially one starts life with a personal 'necessity' consisting of one's heredity and environment. Just as one's environment can become the dominating factor when a person is swayed entirely by social pressures, so, too, can one's natural instincts and feelings come to be the ruling factor of one's life. One becomes an aesthete. The philistine can be said to be governed by his personal necessity insofar as unconscious self-concern and an instinct for self-preservation lie behind his conformity to society. Thus, since children initially accept the social mores unreflectively, an aesthete is likely to be an ex-philistine. At the root of both conditions is natural self-centredness.

Judge William from Part Two of Kierkegaard's *Either/Or* and *Stages on Life's Way* tells us that the aesthetic in a person 'is that by which he spontaneously and immediately is what he is'. The aesthete 'develops with necessity, not in freedom. . . . His soul is like soil out of which grow all sorts of herbs, all with equal claim to flourish; his self consists of this multiplicity, and he has no self that is higher than this.' It is a development 'just like that of a plant'.[4] That is, the only development in an aesthete is in terms of following the natural bent towards what pleases the senses. This process can be unreflective, but it can also be a highly speculated affair.

In *Either/Or*, his first major work, Kierkegaard makes the editor of the book (Victor Eremita) a man who espouses the aesthetic or pleasure-seeking standpoint. Eremita allegedly attempts an impartial presentation of the papers he found, publishing them as two views of life. Kierkegaard makes an aesthete present the papers because such a person is totally unlike the philistine in one respect. The philistine's life is dissipated in its involvement in the surrounding world; he is busy with the business of daily life. The aesthete, on the other hand, detaches himself from his environment in the stance of the shrewd objective observer. Such a one, lacking as he does moral or religious commitment, should be in an ideal position when it comes to the impartial presentation of conflicting views.

Either/Or can make daunting reading because of its composition. Its subtitle 'A Fragment of Life' is especially apposite. It points to the way the content of Part One is structured, indicates the differing life-styles of the characters within the papers and also Eremita's outlook towards both Parts, which he sees as giving the reader a chunk of the real world, insofar as he found and published a hidden cache of apparently private papers. The contents of Part One are highly heterogeneous. After the preface the reader encounters a collection of utterances of varying length from the pen of the young aesthete A. This is followed by an aesthetic analysis of music centred on Mozart's opera *Don Giovanni*, then by a group of papers read by the young aesthete to a society of aesthetes, the *Symparanekromenoi* (The Fellowship of the Dead). The first paper is an analysis of tragedy in ancient and modern drama, with particular reference to the figure of Antigone. The next paper, entitled 'Silhouettes psychological diversion', takes up the theme of reflective sorrow in relation to three betrayed women who have in common their sorrow and deliberation about their betrayal: Marie Beaumarchais from Goethe's *Clavigo*, Donna Elvira from *Don Giovanni* and Margarete from Goethe's *Faust*. The last of the three papers, 'The Unhappiest', attempts to find out who the unhappiest person must be, after which there is an abrupt transition from the *Symparanekromenoi* and the papers to a review of a comedy, an essay on how to defeat boredom and a diary allegedly by another character, a seducer.

At a first reading, the apparent fragmentariness of Part One seems to defy all attempts to treat it as a unity. On top of this is the factor of several layers of strategy. For within *Either/Or* Kierkegaard sends an indirect message to Regine Olsen and takes on the Hegelian philosophers. For Regine, *Either/Or*, especially the Seducer's Diary, is to free her of the relation through the implication that Kierkegaard is a heartless scoundrel she is well rid of.[5] To the Hegelians, *Either/Or* is a message concerning the consequences of the Hegelian standpoint. In a world observed and described from the outside as an unfolding system containing everything in an ongoing necessary process and consisting of various conflicting, but ultimately harmonious, expressions of all existence ('absolute mind'), by what set of ideals should a person live? If one goes along with the norms of one's society like the philistine, one has in fact given one's assent in advance to the prevailing norms of that society. If one is an aesthete, aiming to remain outside considerations of good and bad, except insofar as one can translate these into feelings of what one finds pleasant/ unpleasant, beautiful/ugly, how is one to live in the Hegelian universe? Kierkegaard's aesthete can find no guidance concerning questions to do with career or marriage,[6] which is why Kierkegaard puts him in a society influenced by Hegelian presuppositions. The aesthete 'sees only possibilities everywhere',[7] and in what way can they be objects of real and serious choice? If the historical process is understood as predeterministic necessity, then choice is illusory and one is the victim of predeterministic forces. If, on the other hand, one rejects this and looks upon life as governed by chance, then one can see oneself as governed by meaningless accident. Either way, one is in the grip of one's 'fate', understood as the external events that 'chance' one. Or if one considers the whole picture as one with the individual appearing as a tiny element in the ongoing world-historical process, what meaning can one ascribe to that person's life? It is therefore that the young aesthete bewails loss of meaning, both for the individual and for society as a whole,[8] while later in *Concluding Unscientific Postscript*, Johannes Climacus will criticize the descriptive-objective world-historical picture for the same reasons.[9]

In *Either/Or* Kierkegaard examines the problem from within, showing the perspective of three major aesthetic types. In the aesthetic analysis of Mozart's *Don Giovanni*,[10] what is presented is an objective description of unreflective aestheticism. Don Juan is an instinctive seducer, at the summit of the 'immediate' or spon-taneous erotic stages, yet totally amoral because he unreflectively follows his natural instincts. Reflection, however, presents a threat to the validity of his life-style. In Don Juan it appears at an uncon-scious level, as anxiety in the form of 'demonic zest for life'.[11] Externally, towards the end of his career, it is made specific that there is another option. The Commendatore, returning from the dead, points to a world-view that condemns his activity as breaker of hearts. Don Juan is challenged to think about what he is doing in relation to a power that gives an ethical-religious evaluation of his behaviour. He ends in hell, not because he was an unreflective seducer with a long track-record, but because the Christian world-view he encounters reveals the real state of affairs about things and defines his behaviour as sin. Challenged to reflect, Don Juan refuses to think about his actions. He wishes to retreat to unreflective innocence, even though this is now impossible. Reflection about his behaviour calls for choice, either to repent or to continue his career as a seducer consciously.

Don Giovanni occurs within the context of a Christian culture; thus any reflection about the morality of personal action must take the Christian view of the world into consideration. Kierkegaard's reflective aesthete, the counterpart to Don Juan, thus also occurs within a Christian context. Here, the discussion takes place in the form of direct dialogue between the reader and the aesthete in that we are presented with the diary of a seducer. We move from opera, from music expressing instinctive seduction, to the written word, to emphasis on the method of seduction and the reflective enjoyment of seduction.[12]

Johannes the Seducer has grown up within the context of a Christian culture. He has been brought up within its assumptions. He is also a well-educated and cultivated man. From the diary we learn that Johannes is now aesthete and seducer by choice and calculation. He has 'a pact with the esthetic', and we later learn that he follows 'a categorical imperative – Enjoy'.[13] The form that his enjoyment takes is indulgence in the excitement of the tactics of the chase. Once the girl is hooked the fun is over and it is time to find another. Certainly he is true to the aesthetic ideology as expressed in the essay on 'Rotation of crops',[14] since his diary throughout follows the precepts of that essay. He observes life, avoids commitments to relationships, and especially seeks 'the interesting' in his attempt to keep boredom at bay. Insofar as 'aesthetic' is to be interpreted as enjoyment of the senses and not, for example, as the task of making life beautiful (when he could be seen as responsible for creating the ugliness of Cordelia's tears and Edward's rage), one may well argue that he is faithful in his deeds to the philosophy he says he espouses and thus has 'the idea on his side'. True to his life-style he pursues Cordelia, gets engaged to her, causes her to view engagement and marriage as inferior to permanent free love. She therefore breaks off the engagement in favour of the latter idea, but Johannes abandons her after their first night together.

When we examine Johannes' words, we find that although he despises the philistine convention of engagement, even though he consciously goes along with such social conventions (including churchgoing) to serve his own ends, there is a curious inconsistency concerning his relationship to ethics. He prides himself on distancing himself from people and on living by the aesthetic idea. He tells us he loves Cordelia only in an aesthetic sense. Given this, his self-justification in his diary is surprising. One can leave aside his ironic comment about 'helping' people, when he is clearly manipulating them and cheating them; even the notion of 'developing' Cordelia's innocence and giving her 'experience' can be seen as his genuine belief in what he wants to see. Surprising, however, are aspects of his attempt to present himself to us as an honourable man. Even allowing for an irony that belies his words, Johannes states he has never deceived anyone who has confided in him, that he views marriage as having ethical reality, and that he has never promised marriage to a girl because he has 'a certain respect for the ethical'. Yet Johannes deceives the trusting Edward terribly, and despite his assertion that his engagement to Cordelia is 'simulated', it is hard to see why he need accept or respect the ethical at all, or where the simulation lies. If he views the aesthetic idea the way he says he does, there is no need for excuses for his behaviour. If he genuinely looks for the interesting in life and finds the pursuit of Cordelia an excitement like fox-hunting, then he is true to himself in exploiting and deceiving people and using social institutions, since he consciously steers clear of ethics. Keeping faith in short-term matters is purely to achieve his long-term goals, while to flee from Cordelia's 'revolting' tears is in keeping with his position of aesthetic love. He sees 'eternal' love purely as a collection of intense instants of pleasure rounding off the delights of the chase.[15]

Kierkegaard clearly does not wish us to view Johannes impartially, though. Already in the young aesthete's exposition of *Don Giovanni*, the basic concept of a human is described as spirit, so that Don Juan, despite his aesthetic indifference or amorality, expresses the immorality of the sensuous demonic when viewed against the background of the actuality of spirit. This could be seen as being simply the aesthete's description of the themes of the opera, except that in Victor Eremita's preface, Johannes the Seducer is linked with the notion of the demonic; and the young aesthete A, in his introduction to the diary, speaks of Johannes' scheming mind, of his one day being awakened by conscience and pursued by despair.[16] Thus we are intendedly left with the impression that Johannes, far from consciously choosing one authentic life-style among several others, is a man fundamentally self-deceived and psychologically twisted, deeply alienated from life because of the distance he puts between himself and his self, as well as the world.[17]

Between the two aesthetic positions is to be found that of the young man A. Like Don Juan, he has been unreflective, but gradually various factors cause him to become aware of his situation. If a person, on the basis of enjoyment of what one finds pleasant/ unpleasant, beautiful/ugly, concludes that following one's feelings is a sure guide to the purpose of life, it becomes evident in *Either/Or* that this is not the case. As Kierkegaard tells us in his journals, the aesthetic life of Part One of *Either/Or* is continually shipwrecked on the factor of time.[18] Judge William asserts that every human finds need of a 'life-view' or conception of the meaning and purpose of life, but he sees attempts to make that life-view enjoyment of what is pleasurable/beautiful as doomed to failure. Whether the condition for such enjoyment depends on something external, such as wealth or honour, or on some talent for the existence of which the individual is not responsible, such as a talent for business or art, one is attempting to centre one's life on something that can and does pass away with time. Every aesthetic life-view ends in despair, because it hinges on a condition outside one or outside one's control. While it is true that for a while wealth can be accumulated and talents developed, this is not something that can touch the spiritual potentiality of the self. One lives under an illusion of freedom, an illusion that comes to light when the wealth disappears and the talent fades. What is 'immediately given' or acquired within temporality is subject to the laws of time. Since one's desires also change, even attempting to follow the pattern of changing desires will prove frustrating.[19]

Kierkegaard's young aesthete is shown trying to live aesthetically. In *Either/Or* there is the young aesthete's essay on 'Rotation of crops', the 'theory of social prudence' that recommends various manipulative and evasive tactics for keeping life interesting and enjoyable, holding boredom at bay.[20] In Kierkegaard's pseudonymous work *Repetition*, we have the amusing story of Constantin Constantius' attempt to repeat a previous pleasure trip to Berlin, while in *Stages on Life's Way*, 'In vino veritas' is presented as an example of the tactic of 'recollection', where one consciously 'photographs' special events into one's mind in order to recall them at will later.[21] These tactics are short-term and ultimately doomed to failure as the paper in *Either/Or* on 'The Unhappiest' demonstrates. An unhappy person is one absent from the present self in thought-projections into the past (memory) or future (hope). The unhappiest person combines the two, because that person views the past as lacking significance and the future as holding no reality. Such a one translates the future into the state of something recalled and thus has nothing to hope for.[22] The content of the past must be worth recalling, one must be able to do or experience something good in the present as well as be able to repeat it. Hence the paper is centred on the theme of death, both physical and psychological, in the life that is already written off as finished.[23] The aesthete realizes that in the long run his tactics are no replacement for an answer to the question of how to live in the present.

The apparent fragmentation of Part One of *Either/Or* is thus unified in the central theme of despair. The 'Diapsalmata', the bundle of poetic utterances by the young aesthete, are a refrain on the theme of despair in the face of life's meaninglessness, punctuated by fruitless attempts to enjoy life. The aesthete does not, however, stop with poetic expression of feeling. He also thinks. As an observer of, rather than a participant in, existence, he both poetizes and analyses, constructs and deconstructs. He also arbitrarily experiments with life and people, dabbles in different career possibilities that all seem fundamentally meaningless to him.[24] In this way, he tries to be fate or God in control of the externalities of existence, but his constructiveness is constantly defeated by his misconception of the task and by his analytic destructive irony. Despite this, he seeks to understand life, particularly through his aesthetic analyses of tragedy in the *Symparanekromenoi* papers. Although he sheers off facing up to his personal unhappiness, even at times revels in it and turns to laughter and comedy to help distance himself from life,[25] he is clear that questions about world-views are important since they affect questions of personal life-views and the scope of personal responsibility. With the Seducer's Diary that the young aesthete may have written, he horrifies himself with the picture of the aesthetic life-style taken to a logical extreme.[26] He has jettisoned the Christianity of his childhood in favour of his determination to 'interpret all existence in esthetic categories', but despite himself he feels the need for ethics at least to a certain extent.[27]

The young aesthete attempts to extract the eternal from temporality; this is the source of his despair. The remedy lies in arriving at, and living by, a world-view that can provide attack of the problem at the source. The aesthete's aesthetic (poetic) existence cannot arise from such a world-view in Judge William's eyes because, although poetic ideality is higher than the actual world by virtue of its ideality, it is not something that can be lived. It comes from the given part of the individual's personality (imagination) as talent, and it points away from the actual world, becoming a substitute for it. The poet and artist visualize, create and experience ideals, yet this is always within the aesthetic sphere. The kind of ideal the aesthete needs is one that can be lived. Such an ideal is one that can act as motivation and goal, yet at the same time is already within the person concerned, because it is being actualized in the present. Specifically, the authentic ideal forms part of the actual self as a potential idea of the yet-to-be-actualized self, and is thus the motor of the striving.[28] Fantasized idealities are divorced from the real world and thus cannot make proper contact with the real world. Kierkegaard deals with this theme throughout his authorship, not least in the story of the young man in *Repetition*, whose problem is that the real woman he loves he has transformed in his imagination into a recollected relationship belonging to the past.[29] He is thus through with the relationship before he has embarked upon it.

Either/Or Part One thus presents the entire spectrum of the aesthetic life from unconscious despair to highly reflective despair. Judge William in his diagnosis of the various levels of despair tells the young aesthete that he has reached the last aesthetic life-view, 'despair in thought'. This despair is no longer directed to the failure of temporal objectives. Instead it is a despair resulting from the young man having thought through the vanity of everything, but got no further than that.[30] Occasionally he attempts to drown out the despair by throwing himself into former pleasures; otherwise he is lethargically through with life. The positive with his situation is that he is now totally conscious of his psychological condition. The negative is that he finds life utterly meaningless. The advice Judge William gives the aesthete is based on his own experience. Instead of starting with some dogmatic explanation of his own world-picture, in *Either/Or* Part Two he talks the aesthete through the psychology of his situation in order to put him on the right road from despair.[31]

SOCIETY BUILT ON CHRISTIAN ETHICS

We saw that the philistine unthinkingly followed the norms of society and that the aesthete followed the beckoning of personal desire. The passion of love is chosen particularly to illustrate the life of natural instinct in *Either/Or*, first because of its centrality to human existence. In Part One we are shown love as a passion divorced from duty. With Don Juan there is no consciousness of ethics, with Johannes the Seducer there is total consciousness combined with their rejection. The young aesthete dabbles in ethics but regards duty and love as fundamentally opposed.[32] This is a Kantian polarization,[33] and brings us to the second reason for the book's concern with love – its investigation of the Hegelian emphasis on the harmonization of love and duty, of the wishes of the self with the needs and values of society. We therefore find Judge William arguing for the harmonization of the aesthetic, ethical and religious in such a way that problems with the Hegelian perspective become clear. The Judge's first letter to the young aesthete in *Either/Or* Part Two thus concerns the presentation of marriage as an institution that preserves love and retains the aesthetic element. His second letter deals with how a balance between the life of the passions and the life of ethics is to be achieved in practice.

Despite his use of current Hegelian terminology, Judge William's presuppositions about the nature of the universe are traditional Christian and non-Hegelian. Instead of absolute spirit expressing itself in, and as, the unfolding of the historical universe, Judge William sees a separation between infinite spirit (God), and finite spirit (humans), and is committed to belief in life after death for the individual. The history of the individual is emphasized, and temporality is assigned to the individual finite spirit. The individual is also able to exercise freedom in relation to the necessity of factors of environment and heredity. Thus temporality is a challenge to the individual, yet it contains the possibility of the individual's development and glorification, it exists for the sake of humankind.[34] Seen in this light, Judge William's seemingly dogmatic claim that people have a 'duty to marry' becomes understandable. Rejecting finite reasons given for marriage (such as to have a home or increase the human race),[35] Judge William views the marriage relationship as something lasting and vitally alive, a relationship that combines physical and spiritual love. As he says later in *Stages on Life's Way*, marriage is the 'focal point of life and existence'. It is the essential physical presupposition for the existence of society, but it brings together earthly love – love that concentrates itself on one person – and love finally for everyone. It places the individual in the situation where he or she can bring together personal and social/ civic relationships and also unite a justifiable self-concern for one's own well-being with concern for the needs of others. In this way, the individual and social values or 'the universal', as Judge William calls it, are brought together. There is a duty to love and to stabilize the relationship in marriage, which unites the life of feeling and instinct with free purpose after reflection and in relation to the needs of society.[36]

In his first letter to the young aesthete in *Either/Or* Part One, Judge William raises the question of what love is, since the aesthete's view is clearly that love is purely an emotional matter. In his review of *The First Love*, the young aesthete exposes the irony of Scribe's farce because it shows up the first passion as temporary or illusory. This illusoriness is seen also as a reason for the contemporary irony about romantic love. Romantic love is based on the transitoriness of feeling and beauty yet is conscious of being an eternal commitment. The romantic novel and play show young lovers fighting temporal obstacles to the 'happy ever after' ending and omit the lifelong relationship. Judge William criticizes the replacement of romantic love with temporary affairs or marriages of convenience, for these divorce love and duty in unacceptable ways. While approving the sense of love and striving belonging to romantic love, the Judge sees its weakness in resting the weight of the relationship on transitory feeling and on the overcoming of external problems.[37] Judge William argues that it is through ethics that marriage becomes the aesthetic expression for love, providing, as it does, a different understanding of 'eternity'. For the aesthete, to eternalize something means to repeat some external or externally related experience in some way within temporality. Since such repetition proves a failure, the aesthetic notion of eternity turns out to be false. For Judge William, life within an ethical framework changes the conception of eternity.

Within ethics 'eternity' means that one eternalizes or continues in ('repeats') the relationship despite changes of mood and external situation.[38] From this perspective, purely sensuous beauty acquires the permanent beauty of ethics and the resulting development of the partnership with the years. Thus a relationship that began on the basis of spontaneous attraction is purposively taken further by free choice even when the aesthetic elements of the relationship have faded. Ethics have primacy in relation to both the aesthetic and the religious life, because the aesthetic life without ethics proves frustrating and destructive, while a religious life divorced from ethics, and hence society, is a self-oriented aesthetic wallowing in spontaneous religious feelings.[39]

In his second letter to the young aesthete in *Either/Or* Part Two, Judge William turns to the all-important question of what duty is. Here, it is important to see at the outset that he is telling the aesthete how to get started on a moral, as opposed to aesthetic, existence. He is fully aware that the aesthete had the same upbringing as himself, therefore does not lack an intellectual understanding of what morality entails. Also, to embark on a discussion of ethics would be merely to provide the aesthete with further interesting and hence purely aesthetic intellectual activity. Hence he starts from the aesthete's psychological situation of 'thought despair'.

Initially one is surprised that the Judge should tell the aesthete to 'choose despair', and some of the Hegelian-flavoured language (the reapplication of Hegelian terms to the individual) used to describe the psychology of the move to an ethical life-style can prove difficult for the reader. For when one chooses despair one chooses 'the absolute', which is the self in its 'eternal validity', and what is chosen is one's self and it exists already, but it also does not exist yet, because one is not creating oneself, one is born as free spirit out of the principle of contradiction.[40]

To put it simply, the despairing aesthete tries to flee his despair and get rid of it by trying different aesthetic pursuits to drown it out. Or else he tries to trace its source to some finite lack of something. When he finally *chooses* despair, he faces up to it. It is a choice of the self as guilty, a choice of the self that is repentance of the self, an abandonment of asserting the validity of the self in its present condition. Especially it is the choice to choose or make a distinction between good and evil, right and wrong, to live according to those categories. This is something one already begins to do in the initial choice of despair, since one accepts the idea that the self is not good as it is, instead of fleeing from despair as an unpleasant psychological experience. It is also a choice of the self in its 'eternal validity', because it is a taking up of the reins of one's life, a new purposiveness, or use of will. The decision to use one's personal freedom in taking responsibility for one's self, in looking for real possibilities in life as tasks instead of playing with various possibilities from an aesthetic perspective, leads one to the development of one's spiritual or eternal self, the self that exists thus far only potentially.

The choice of despair is therefore the way into needed self-knowledge or 'transparency' – clarity about oneself – and it is the initial choice between living by the categories of good and evil or remaining in aesthetic indifference/amorality. Choice of ethics also brings the individual in contact with God the 'eternal power'. Instead of being absorbed in one's life on a moment-by-moment basis, one now has an overview of one's life and, not least, its connectedness with one's environment. The contrast can also be seen in the opposing movements of the closed-up, self-seeking life of a person like Johannes the Seducer, to take the extreme instance of the aesthetic life, and the new active involvement with people around one as individuals in their own right. Since the new life-style brings about development of personality, the potential new self is gradually actualized in the ethical life-style and one uncovers a new self that makes itself apparent to one's neighbours. The aesthete now has new categories by which to live, and even though the new-born ethicist may make mistakes on the ethical path, because the personality is now a consolidated consciousness instead of being a fragmented personality, and because in the continuing choice between right and wrong the new ethicist wishes to do the right thing, he or she has a purity of intention that forms a link with God and at the same time acts as a guide that can be used to judge actions after they have been performed.

At first this psychological description of becoming ethical rings true, especially when we also learn that beauty and the emotions are not thrown out in favour of some kill-joy existence. On the contrary, the aesthetic is only dethroned from its position as total controller of one's life. Similarly a person's religious life is brought back on track in relation to community life in the real world, while the more one tries to do the right thing, the more one will have ethical experience as guide by which to check actions in retrospect. Contact with God is also firmly associated with the necessity of ethics. One can add to this that the core of Judge William's ethical advice can be seen as extremely useful if one has to explain to a pleasure-seeking aesthete what 'ethics' means. The ethical is 'the choice by which one chooses good and evil or rules them out'. Such advice could be given in any culture in relation to every type of ethic or ethical situation.

Yet this very universality is what causes difficulties, since it appears to imply a relativity of ethical norms. Judge William himself recognizes the problem that 'at times a people has pronounced something to be sacred and lawful that in the eyes of another people was abominable and evil'. 'Duty itself is unstable . . . laws can be changed.' The problem of the content of the 'good' and the 'evil' proves fatal to viewing Kierkegaard's authorship in terms of three stages of which 'the ethical' is the second, for Judge William's solution takes us down dangerous paths. He suggests that the point about the ethical is not the external but the internal: 'however much the external is changed, the moral value of the action remains the same.' In reply to the objection put forward that 'civilized nations made it the children's duty to care for their parents' but 'savages practiced the custom of putting their aged parents to death', the Judge replies that 'the question remains whether the savages intend to do something evil by this. The ethical always resides in this consciousness.'[41]

This insistence on the good intention as controlling guide concerning what the 'right' and the 'good' are is clearly of little help. So far we have learned that life does not work for one's self or for others in terms of living solely for one's personal self-oriented desires. In other words, any form of ethical or personal egoism has been shown to be ruled out on practical grounds of results to oneself and others, but where do we go from there? Are we to start from a deontological ethics (start from the rules or eternally valid laws) or from a teleological ethics (here understood as the consequences of actions determining an action's worth or correctness)? If ethical or personal egoism is to be ruled out, should I espouse utilitarianism (all have an equal claim) or altruism (put others first)? How does Judge William avoid validating the Nazi who is honestly convinced he is doing right, or the Brave New World scenario of Aldous Huxley?

The answer to this question is given by Kierkegaard throughout his authorship, but in *Either/Or* the answer is clear if one keeps in mind the distinction between the practical advice on how to start being ethical and the content of the code of ethics. One must also remember that the authentic religious life goes intrinsically with ethical considerations and not with aesthetic ones. In *Either/Or* Kierkegaard takes two contemporary life-styles: that of the person who long ago lost contact with childhood Christianity and that of the ordinary godly Christian. Judge William's ethics are Christian ethics and validly the community ethics in Danish Protestant Lutheranism. He does not need to give the aesthete concrete ethical rules because both the aesthete and Kierkegaard's contemporary reader know them by heart. Thus it is already given that Judge William commends a deontological ethics and an altruistic life-style that he makes clear is to be directed towards the good of everyone. Both the Judge and the aesthete are fully aware that their society's ethical code books are the Bible and, for daily use, Balle's catechism with its long chapter on duties. So Judge William tells the aesthete to regard his letters as 'notes to Balle's Catechism', and declares that 'with the ethical it is not a matter of the multiplicity of duty but of its intensity', of the acquisition of a profound sense of duty.[42]

Since the Bible contains a number of ethical prescriptions it is important to sum them up briefly here, because the difference between Judge William's understanding of Christian ethics and Kierkegaard's, later in the authorship, depends on the emphasis one places on the different groups of prescriptions. From the Old Testament the obvious code is the ten commandments, also laws containing the 'eye for eye' or 'like for like' and prescriptions addressed to community life. In the New Testament there is the Old Testament summary of the law – love of God and neighbour with short summaries of some of the ten commandments – and the Golden Rule: 'Always treat others as you would like them to treat you',[43] which in Matthew is related to Old Testament prescription. Also in the New Testament are the Beatitudes addressed to the community as individuals, e.g. 'Blessed are those who show mercy', along with something different. Jesus intensifies the law. For example, the prescription against adultery is intensified to a prescription against even entertaining the thought of it; nurturing anger appears to be just as bad as murder. An eye for an eye becomes turning the other cheek and giving cloak as well as abandoning claim on the stolen shirt; love of neighbour and hate of enemy becomes the injunction to love enemies and pray for persecutors. The Golden Rule is also intensified in that it is used to encourage love of enemies – how you treat others is how God will treat you – and it is connected with the thought that just as God's goodness is boundless, so must there be no limit placed on the human doing of good. Also, blessing is attached to persecution for the sake of Jesus and future woe to the currently rich and happy. Finally, there is the concrete example of God's limitless goodness in the life and death of Jesus, together with injunctions to follow and imitate him, take up one's cross, be ready to sell and give up everything, even family, for his sake.[44]

From the above, it can be seen that one can divide the various injunctions up into two main categories: the doing of what is right and good according to prescriptions that leave room for a prospering life in a community setting, and a doing of goodness that goes unlimitedly beyond prescription and, not only leaving no room for staying with daily life in community setting, sets one in conflict with the community. The one is not necessarily an alternative to the other (one might be in community as a member of a strict religious order), but it might be in a persecution situation. It is in a persecution, or conflict with community, situation that eternal life as a future goal for the individual may be strongly emphasized. In either situation the New Testament commendation of altruism could be interpreted mildly (leaving room for personal ethics-based enjoyment of temporality) or in the strong sense of total renunciation for God and others. No limit is to be placed on the doing of good, but it is clear that the community situation will affect the possibilities open to one. In a well-functioning society total altruism might not be needed, even if one personally set no limits on one's willingness. Judge William clearly finds himself in this situation, which is why, although he is content to practise a mild altruism, he does not, when rejoicing in temporality as God's gift, fail to note that temporality 'always retains in itself an element of an *ecclesia pressa* [oppressed church]'.[45] Also, while he stresses duty and the apparent agreement between individual and community rule (the universal) in the doing of duty, he finds place for justified exceptions, and so much so that in *Stages on Life's Way* he is prepared to let the validity of the ethical-religious exception displace the priority of marriage as duty, thus making room at least in theory for total New Testament renunciation.[46]

That Judge William is undoubtedly a committed Christian is made patently clear in *Either/Or*. He acknowledges belief in God and the incarnation of Christ. He is a regular churchgoer. He reads the Bible and commentaries and appears to be fairly well-versed in the teachings of the Church. He emphasizes the importance of the Christian virtues and prescriptions, relies on God's grace, believes in immortality and final judgement after death.[47] He also speaks of Balle's catechism as of a primer still having validity, after he learnt its contents as a child.[48] Furthermore, Balle's catechism makes its presence strongly felt throughout the Judge's writings. Reference to God as the 'eternal power' is inspired by Balle's catechism, as is the Judge's reference to immortality of the soul and final judgement, and his emphasis on duties to God, self and neighbour. The mild sense of sin to be found in Balle ('Experience shows that people are not as good as they ought to be') is also reflected in Judge William's mild sense of sin (and he uses the word 'sin', not just 'guilt'), but with this difference: he includes with his letters to the aesthete a sermon by a pastor from pietistic Jutland on the theme of always being wrong in relation to God. 'The truth that builds up' a person contains precisely the sense of limitlessness in relation to the standard of goodness to be found with the stricter New Testament injunctions. Thus, although the sermon, like Judge William and Balle, operates with a mild notion of sin, the sermon's emphasis on 'always' being in the wrong removes a limit to what the good requires and how one stands in relation to it.[49]

Bishop Balle wrote his *Catechism in the Evangelical-Christian Religion Arranged for Use in the Danish Schools* towards the end of the eighteenth century. It became a best-seller, remaining in use until 1856. Balle, especially inspired by Martin Luther's Small Catechism, planned his own in eight chapters, of which a large chapter was devoted to 'duties'.[50] Each section of each chapter is plentifully supplied with Bible references. The chapter on duties states in its introduction that our duty is to do whatever God has commanded us to do. Our general duties are concretely stated to be the ten commandments, which Balle says contain duties every person in every age should follow, because they promote the welfare of ourselves and others. The entire Law of God, according to Christ, aims to promote and strengthen an active love among people to God, self and neighbour.[51]

Balle starts his discussion of duties with a section on duties to God. Among other things, this section encourages love of God above everything. We should rejoice and have confidence in him because he can and will promote our temporal as well as spiritual and eternal welfare. The God-fearing citizen, who has a duty to attend Church on Sunday, praises and extols God in prayer and song and in conversation with others. The next section of the chapter deals with duties to ourselves. We are to love ourselves so we can care adequately for our soul's blessedness, our body, and our temporal welfare. We should often think about death (though not in a sorrowful or anxious manner) so we are always ready for it whenever it comes. Concerning care for our temporal welfare, it is in order to strive to increase one's prosperity through hard work, but not to make the pursuit of wealth the goal of our existence. We may also aim to be honoured, respected and trusted by others, but only through being upright and honest and cultivating Christian humility. We may enjoy life and the good things of temporality, but pleasures must not be the goal of our lives. In the section on duties to our neighbour, we have a duty to love the neighbour as genuinely as we love ourselves and follow the Golden Rule, which means that we should care about the neighbour's body and soul and temporal welfare as much as our own. We should not hate or persecute our enemies, but rather seek to help them as our neighbour, though we may seek protection against them through the official laws. Balle gives detailed injunctions about our behaviour to our neighbour, including good business ethics and equality in our regard for all. There are special duties for husbands and wives, parents and children, masters and servants, government and subjects, teachers (here including pastors) and pupils.

Noteworthy in Balle's chapter on duties are firstly the injunctions not to make pleasure the goal of one's life and to avoid seducing others to do wrong, both of which suggest the characterizations of the aesthetic life in *Either/Or* Part One. Secondly, under care for the neighbour's soul, we are urged to take care of our neighbour's guidance concerning the achievement of a better life in the next world through helpful education, advice, loving warning and good example, which is surely what Judge William is made to do, and what Kierkegaard can be seen as doing in the bulk of his authorship. Thirdly, the injunction about equality of regard for all, and the close link between love of God and neighbour, not only appears in *Either/Or* Part Two, it is expanded upon intensively later in Kierkegaard's *Works of Love*. Also in Balle there is reference to marriage, but it looks as if in Kierkegaard's time the emphasis had shifted from Balle's emphasis on sexuality within the confines of a monogamous relationship to the idea that marriage was a duty and the meaning of life.[52]

Judge William therefore centres the individual's relation to God, self and neighbour on the ethical. He shows how the individual can come into the foundation God-relationship underlying all other relationships through the initial ethical choice that puts the individual into 'an immediate relation to God', but also with the neighbour 'in the closest connection and most intimate relation with an outside world'.[53] This enables the Judge to present 'duties to the self' adequately so that such duties are not confounded with aesthetic self-love. He shows (as does Balle) that there is a difference between the self-love of the egoistic aesthete and a 'self-love that claims for its own self the same as it claims for everyone else's self'. Just as Balle sees nothing selfish in being 'duty-bound to love ourselves', take care of ourselves so we can also help others, so, too, does the Judge see making the self a 'task' a necessary priority, not as something isolated, but always in connection with God and neighbour. The self that is 'the objective' develops 'the personal, the civic, the religious virtues', moves from self-isolation to consciousness of personal and community history. The individual is in a continuous state of relational movement. One finds oneself in relation to one's neighbour through discovery of the ethical and God, and one discovers God through one's ethical relations with one's neighbour.[54]

Thus, in both Judge William's letters and in Balle, life is to be enjoyed as a community of individuals under God, caring for each other. The community's ethics are Protestant Lutheran Christian, especially as mediated by Bishop Balle. Judge William does, however, leave room for development beyond the ethical prescriptions of Balle, and he himself develops (*Stages on Life's Way*) towards viewing total Christian altruism as higher than the mild Christian altruism to which he has dedicated himself.[55]

Notes

1. A Danish word originally used contemptuously, especially of the uncultured classes. Kierkegaard takes up this term with an emphasis on the element of absorption and lack of self-awareness.
2. SV, I, p. 343 (EOI); VII, p. 477 (CUP); XI, pp. 153–4 (SD); XII, pp. 466–7 (FSE/JY); XIV, pp. 244–5 (AC, pp. 205–6).
3. PAP, X,2 A 390 (JP).
4. SV, II, pp. 161, 201–2, cf. 206 (EOII).
5. PAP, X,1 A 266; X,5 A 153 (JP).
6. SV, II, pp. 35–7, 150, 202 (EOII).
7. SV, II, p. 226 (EOII).
8. SV, I, pp. 14–15, 119 (EOI). Judge William (SV, II, p. 18 (EOII)) also bewails the disintegration of society in similar words.
9. SV, VII, pp. 128–31 (CUP).
10. SV, I, pp. 66–112 (EOI).
11. SV, I, p. 108 (EOI).
12. SV, I, pp. 275–412, cf. x–xi, 80, 87–8 (EOI).
13. SV, I, p. 404, 261 (EOI); VI, p. 71 (SLW). The young aesthete also declares enjoyment to be the purpose of life.
14. SV, I, pp. 257–72 (EOI).
15. Seducer's Diary, references: SV, I, pp. 343, 350–3, 277, 329–331, cf. 357, 364, 371–2, 378–9, 320, 341, 336, 404–5, 411–12 (EOI).
16. SV, I, pp. 47, 71–2, x–xi, 275–82 (EOI).
17. SV, I, p. 277 (EOI).
18. SV, I, pp. 261–2 (EOI); PAP, IV A 213 (JP); cf. SV, VII, pp. 213–14 (CUP).

19. SV, II, pp. 162–7, 175, 201, 211 (EOII).
20. SV, I, pp. 257–72 (EOI).
21. As is also the case with repetition, recollection here can be seen as an aesthetic parody of ethical and religious recollection.
22. Such a person is like the young aesthete who, when he is about to go on a pleasant carriage drive, imagines the course of the entire outing before setting out. He has already done the journey in his mind, finds it meaningless and has nothing to hope for from undertaking it. See SV II, 182–3, cf. 175 (EOII).
23. SV, I, pp. 191–203 (EOI). It is to be noted that Judge William also points out (SV, II, p. 129 (EOII)) the aesthetic misrelationship to hope and recollection. The healthy individual should live in hope and recollection, but together in the present.
24. SV, I, pp. xiv–xvi, 22–4 (EOI); SV, II, pp. 150–1, 202 (EOII).
25. SV, I, pp. 27, 204–51 (EOI). 'Rotation of crops' (SV, I, pp. 257–72 (EOI)) is a light essay, cf. also PAP, IV A 216 (JP); SV, VII, pp. 212–14 (CUP).
26. SV, I, pp. 137, x–xi (EOI). Whether or not he is a real person in *Either/Or*, Johannes the Seducer seems to become a real character later in *Stages on Life's Way*, 'In vino veritas', SV, VI, pp. 70–8 (SLW).
27. SV, II, pp. 209, 136 (EOII).
28. SV, II, pp. 189, 245, 231–2, 124 (EOII); SV, VI, p. 394 (SLW); SV, XII, pp. 173–9 (PC); SV, XI, p. 144 (SD); cf. PAP, IX A 382 (JP).
29. SV, III, pp. 175–86 (FT/R).
30. SV, II, pp. 175–6 (EOII).
31. SV, II, p. 187 (EOII).
32. SV, II, pp. 133–5, 243 (EOII).
33. For the philosopher Immanuel Kant (1724–1804), moral action lies in overcoming arbitrary non-rational desires and doing duty for its own sake. Hegel agrees with Kant insofar as he thought arbitrary desires were unfreely governed by natural and social forces. One's actions should therefore be based solely on reason. He disagrees with Kant, however, about the divorce between reason and desire. In Hegel's view, desire and reason harmonize because the rational society fosters desires beneficial to the community and takes the individual's wishes into consideration. One knows one's duties and wants to do them. Since world history is the necessary progress or unfolding of the consciousness of freedom, then on Hegel's view the good and free society will inevitably come about. See Peter Singer, *Hegel* (Oxford University Press, 1983), esp. ch. 3, pp. 24–44. Gardiner (*Kierkegaard*, p. 48) sees 'Hegelian overtones' in *Either/Or* Part Two, in the 'progressive spiritual movement' from the aesthetic to the ethical life, concluding that the early Kierkegaard is more Hegelian than the later Kierkegaard. This need not follow, however, since Kierkegaard here is depicting a committed Christian in nineteenth-century Hegelian-influenced Denmark. Judge William does not treat the ethical life as totally trouble-free, as Gardiner also points out (pp. 54, 87), while the Judge's Christian universe is radically different from the Hegelian world process model.
34. SV, II, pp. 224, 56–7, 289 (EOII).

35. SV, II, pp. 220, 270, 273, 58–81 (EOII).
36. SV, VI, pp. 112, 98 (SLW); SV, II, pp. 57, 235–6, 243 (EOII).
37. SV, II, pp. 16–26, 125–6 (EOII).
38. SV, II, pp. 268, 128 (EOII).
39. SV, II, pp. 215–24 (EOII). It should be noted that Judge William admits lack of competence on the subject of mysticism, while his concrete example of catastrophe in such a life is not Christian. His description best fits the pseudo-mysticism rejected by spiritual literature on the subject.
40. SV, II, pp. 189–96, cf. 151–4, 160–2, 185, 198, 200, 202, 206, 208, 213–14, 216, 222–3, 225 (EOII).
41. SV, II, pp. 236–8 (EOII).
42. SV, II, pp. 290, 238–40 (EOII).
43. Exodus 20:3–17; cf. chs 20 – 22, 34; Leviticus; Deut 5:6–21; chs 6, 12 – 31; Matt 22:37–40; Mark 12:29–31; Luke 10:27; cf. Deut 6:4; Mark 10:19; Luke 18:20; Matt 7:1–2, 12; cf. Luke 6:31.
44. Matt 5:3–11; cf. Luke 6:20–21; Matt 5:27–28, 21–22, 38–40, 43–44; cf. Luke 6:27–38 and, e.g., Exod 21:24; Luke 6:22–38; Matt 5:48; cf. 5:20 (one must be far better than the scribes and Pharisees, the epitome of good law-keepers); Matt 16:24–26; Mark 8:34–35; Luke 14:26–27; cf. Mark 9:35; Luke 9:23, 25; Matt 19:21; Mark 10:21; Luke 18:22; cf. Rom 8:29; Phil 2:5–15; Col 3:9–14.
45. SV, II, p. 224 (EOII).
46. SV, II, pp. 236, 294–8 (EOII); SV, VI, pp. 161–72, 98, 104 (SLW).
47. SV, II, pp. 5, 14–15, 37–8, 55, 56, 64–5, 83–6, 111–12, 153, 184, 186, 194, 197–9, 203, 213, 220, 229, 232, 242, 281–2, 288, 289, 291 (EOII).
48. SV, II, pp. 239, 242, 290 (EOII).
49. SV, II, pp. 152–3, 242, 288–9, 291, 238, 193–4, 201, 213, 216, 301–18 (EOII), and index references to sin; cf. BALLE, ch. 6, III, paras 2, 3, 6; ch. 8, paras 2, 3, 5; ch. 6; ch. 3, para. 1.
50. For a detailed discussion of the background to Balle's catechism see Julia Watkin, 'Judge William – a Christian?' in Robert L. Perkins (ed.), *International Kierkegaard Commentary: Either/Or* (Macon, GA: Mercer University Press, 1995), ch. 5.

BALLE is structured as follows:

I. God and his attributes
   How we learn to know God
   What Scripture teaches us about God generally
   What Scripture teaches us about God's nature and attributes
II. God's works
   What Scripture teaches us about creation and the created things
   What Scripture teaches us about God's providence and preservation of the created things
III. On man's corruption through sin
IV. On man's reclamation from sin through Jesus Christ, God's Son
V. On sinners' participation in the mercy and blessedness acquired by Christ
VI. On the fruits of faith in a holy life ('On duties')
VII. On aids to strengthening faith and growth in godliness

God's Word
Vigilance and prayer
The sacrament of baptism
The sacrament of Holy Communion
VIII. On man's final condition
Short summary of the Evangelical-Christian religion's main doctrines

51. BALLE, ch. 6, introductory section.
52. PAP, XI,1 A 226, cf. XI,1 A 129, 169; XI,2 A 154, 238; VIII,1 A 190; X,1 A 440; IX A 245; X,3 A 293 (JP).
53. SV, II, pp. 152, 216 (EOII); BALLE, ch. 6, A I, 3a, b, and para. 9.
54. SV, II, pp. 153, 243, 235–6, 193–4 (EOII); BALLE, ch. 6, A I, 6, and B, III, 1, a, cf. C, 'On duties to one's neighbour'.
55. SV, VI, p. 161 (SLW).

6

Christianity in conflict with culture

THE TENSION OF DYING TO THE WORLD

In *Either/Or*, Judge William presupposes the validity of Christian ethics as 'the universal', binding on all who opt for the ethical-religious, as opposed to the aesthetic, life. While he views the individual's ethical situation generally as being a happy conformity of desire with duty, he accepts that there may be exceptional situations in which the individual cannot fulfil his or her duty. Such exceptions are still within ethics, however, since the individual in question recognizes the validity of the unfulfillable duty, and of the community's ethical code. Similarly, when the Judge in *Stages on Life's Way* reluctantly accepts the justified renouncer of marriage as one doing something higher than marrying, such renunciation is still within the confines of Christian ethics as a possibility presented by Scripture to the individual. Yet Judge William's reluctance to accept such renunciation is justified. As the Judge (and Kierkegaard himself in his journals) fully realizes, celibacy as a universal precept would cause the human race to die out[1] and thus remove the presupposition for the very existence of ethics and any form of altruism in relation to other humans. As a counsel of perfection, celibacy has its place as part of a specifically religious call.

If we look at the matter from the point of view of altruism in relation to others (and to God as the primary relationship for all individuals in the community), then it is easy to see that altruism can vary radically in its intensity. Judge William espouses a mild God-based Christian altruism that leaves space for unselfish personal enjoyment as long as this is consonant with duty. Within community life in temporality, however, even though there can be instances of extreme self-sacrifice and heroism, there in fact always remains a natural self-orientation belonging to nature: one belongs to one's own family, one's own community, one's own race. Thus, the more one deepens a life of altruism, the more there will come to be a tension between the life of nature and the life of spirit, which, as exemplified in the life of Jesus, is one of total self-renunciation, including the possibility of death for others. So in the light of self-renunciation as ideality, Christianity can be seen as the life of the spirit at variance with the life of the flesh.[2] Judge William would unite earthly and spiritual love,[3] love for one person and love for all, but there are intrinsic conflict points. To take but one example, it is accepted that the duty to care for one's children must come before the duty to care for those needing food, clothes and education in areas of famine. The duty to care for both children and the starving are manageable on Judge William's application of Christianity – but only up to a point. If the Judge had to choose between letting his child starve or letting a stranger starve, he would feed his child and as a parent ought to do so. Duty as well as love insists upon this, given his responsibility for his child coming into the world. To be freed from that particular responsibility to devote oneself totally to the world's needy calls for the Mother Teresas and not the Judge Williams. Judge William participates totally in temporal relationships, the monastics in the world represent a different form of total participation that requires renunciation of marriage and personal family. The individual must therefore choose his or her form of participation. Nor does Kierkegaard, when he is not beating his contemporaries with the rod of ideality, attempt to say which altruistic or self-renouncing ideal that person should choose.[4]

The mild putting of others first is thus something that can intensify into a total religious self-denial for others and God. In *Concluding Unscientific Postscript*, Climacus speaks of the Judge William ethical life-style as one in which 'the underlying self is used to surmount and assert itself'. The ethicist lives consciously by the Christian code in its mildness, overcomes self-centredness and serves others, but still has an area of natural self-orientation in the things that belong to his or her life. The one with a more God-centred life, however, is defined as 'turned inward in self-annihilation before God',[5] or dies to the world. In other words, the individual still lives within the usual relationships of temporality but is intent on fulfilling the pattern of religious ideality (whether Christ, Torah or Qur'an), and is detached from personal relationships in the sense that godly neighbour love is opposed to preferential love, and one's spouse must first and foremost be one's neighbour. In the course of this intensified God-relationship, though, the individual discovers suffering in the discovery of human inability to fulfil ideality – or even successfully to apply and pass the constant 'resignation' test to check that there is nothing finite, no feature of temporal possessions, he or she would not be ready to give up for the God-relationship and the accompanying eternal blessedness. Dying to one's life in the ordinary ethical-temporal sense, to preferential love, and having an absolute relation to God with all else viewed as relative to it, calls for an enormous effort that in one sense adds up to nothing because, apart from the difficulty that a finite human can never fulfil a demand to be or act like the infinite good or God, this realization of the non-fulfillability is the factual one the individual needs to arrive at.[6]

Far from being a negative assessment that seems pessimistic towards making an effort (why bother?) and towards a proper evaluation of temporality, the religious intensification points the way towards dealing with others unselfishly, as individuals in their own right with their own needs. In seriously following the admonitions in Kierkegaard's religious discourses, especially *Purity of Heart* and *Works of Love*, the individual, even if unable to fulfil their infinite scope, becomes aware of the infinite nature of the ideals of love and goodness (that it is hard enough to love the beloved, let alone the enemy), understands why those regarded as holy and saintly see themselves as wretched sinners.[7] To sum up, the individual is living according to such admonitions and precepts (but not legalistically), and grows, morally- and spiritually-speaking, but can never fulfil them in the sense of complete them. On the contrary, the summit of such a life is the discovery that the truth of subjectivity or living religiously – as opposed to intellectual assent to religious propositions – is 'untruth'. The maximum of human striving brings the individual to a profound sin-consciousness.[8] Such a realization is catastrophic for the individual lacking the possibility of divine forgiveness and grace, since, on Kierkegaard's view of the individual's need to develop the eternal or spiritual self ethical-religiously, that eternal self cannot be so developed or completed.[9]

It is here that Kierkegaard lays weight on two further aspects of the specifically religious element of the ethical-religious life. First, since the striving individual can in fact do nothing to fulfil his or her own eternal potentiality, there is a switch from emphasis on Jesus the ethical-religious pattern to Jesus the Saviour bringing God's grace and forgiveness. Instead of the essentiality for humans to actualize their eternal, ethical-religious selves through repetition or continuity of the ethical-religious life, God makes good human deficiency through the coming of Christ to the world. As the argument of both *Philosophical Fragments* and *Concluding Unscientific Postscript* shows,[10] the difference between Jesus and a figure such as Socrates is this: that Socrates is merely the occasion by which someone brings knowledge of, and involvement with, the eternal to consciousness, whereas the work of Jesus acts as the restoration of someone's ability to learn at all. The believer's encounter with Christ is, of course, double-edged, since in experiencing Jesus as God's likeness, the believer correspondingly also experiences the contrast of acute sin-consciousness.

Second, the limitation of the human mind is radically illustrated in *Concluding Unscientific Postscript*. Hegel, like others before and after him, attempted to explain all existence in one universe of objective knowledge. Kierkegaard attacks this god-like perspective as a false one for humans. He views such human 'omniscience' as a self-deception.[11] Such an attitude is spiritually dangerous because it takes the individual away from the ethical-religious life. While there is nothing wrong with objective knowledge in its proper place, what humans grasp is always an approximation to truth, never truth in its entirety. The illusion of total knowledge gives humans a false sense of ultimate power and control, encourages a casual attitude towards truth as something propositional. As a body of objective knowledge it does not call for any particular personal life-style, and the subjective-action aspect of ethics is not genuinely included in the big picture, distanced as it is from the observing individual.

In *Concluding Unscientific Postscript* Kierkegaard's Climacus exercises the individual in a proper recognition of the finitude of the human mind, which, if allowed to play the role of God, becomes a hindrance to the God-relationship through the displacement of God in the individual's life. In *Concluding Unscientific Postscript* and also the earlier *Philosophical Fragments* (1844), Kierkegaard therefore undermines the attempt to gain philosophical and historical certainty in the religious life. He shows the attempt to be based on the false idea that faith is inferior to knowledge, whereas much of what passes for knowledge is in fact hypothesis to which we have given the assent of faith. Belief in propositions, however, is distinct from the existential faith-commitment to an ethical-religious life-style, and the propositional form of belief can distract from the existential commitment in a number of ways that can seriously blinker the individual in the endeavour to enter into and deepen the God-relationship.[12]

The prospective believer starts with an intellectual objective uncertainty concerning God's existence, an objective uncertainty that also attaches itself to a wide range of things that one mistakenly accepts as certain.[13] Kierkegaard also makes a clear distinction between objective knowledge as truth, in relation to which a person is in intellectual truth if the knowledge in question is in fact true, and subjective truth, in which the truth lies in the authenticity of the individual's ethical-religious behaviour, even if that individual has some erroneous conceptions about the nature of God (such as that God is a stone idol). For the religious believer there is thus a 'paradox' or seemingly contradictory contrast between the certainty or persistence of his or her ethical-religious commitment and the intellectual objective uncertainty surrounding the object of belief. As if this were not enough, Kierkegaard makes Climacus go on to the equivalent of an intellectual dying to the world in his presentation of Jesus as the incarnate God.

To try to understand God in terms of objective knowledge (and even think one can do so or has done so) is to enclose God and religion within the sphere of the finite intellect. Hence Climacus is made to keep the door open, so to speak, by showing a God revealed negatively to human reason as the limit of reason as it strives to reach beyond the frontier of the known. Additionally, within a Christian culture, a person is referred to the figure of the historical Jesus, where, apart from the impossibility of arriving at historical certainty, the individual is confronted with reports of belief claims, namely that the man Jesus is identical with God, that the eternal becomes incarnate within the temporal world at a particular moment of history. These claims, as Kierkegaard-Climacus points out, are not merely propositions subject to objective uncertainty, they go against human reason, since, as we saw in Chapter 3, the claim being made is that the eternal can change – be born into the temporal order of things – on top of which comes the 'offence' of identifying God with a poor, serving teacher who died the death of a criminal. This calls not for faith in the light of objective uncertainty, but, in addition, an intensified faith against the understanding; that is, continuation in the Christian life not only in spite of the extra intellectual problems, but making sure that one has grasped what they are. Faith in this case – in the 'absurd' – is not the acceptance of any old nonsense, but a crucifixion of the understanding or a despair of the reason (on a parallel with Judge William's call for despair of the aesthetic life) by which one abandons the intellectual struggle in favour of a deeper level of existential commitment. One has discovered that one lacks any means of proving the Christian doctrine of redemption.[14]

With the notion of 'offence' Kierkegaard also gets rid of Lessing's problem, the problem of *Philosophical Fragments* and *Concluding Unscientific Postscript*, namely, whether one can rest the question of one's eternal blessedness on an historical claim. Kierkegaard's solution is to deny that one can intellectually, but assert that it is possible through faith. Whether a contemporary of Jesus or a late-twentieth-century citizen, the prospective believer is in the same situation of seeing the contradiction of a man claiming to be God. The sacred history (accounts by believers) that has come down to us can do no more than be an occasion for a modern person to accept or reject the claim, and according to Climacus, what in fact happens is that Christ himself makes it possible for the individual to believe in him, and then the individual is free to accept or reject him. In this way, the condition of the believer is still one of being able to do nothing of himself. We can here note Kierkegaard-Climacus' insistence that the previous religiousness of dying to the world is an essential presupposition for commitment in faith to Jesus as saviour.[15]

Care needs to be taken, however, concerning Kierkegaard-Climacus' statements about Jesus and the incarnation. Kierkegaard's tactic, on the one hand, is to emphasize the 'offence' of Christianity in order to stir his contemporaries into taking Christianity seriously instead of carelessly for granted. On the other hand, Climacus' statements are directed to *human* reason. That is, within the context of the limitations of human reason, it is perfectly possible to present Christian doctrine in terms of opposing doctrinal statements, where the presenter starts with assumptions about the nature of eternity and can then proceed to show that contradiction is implied. A person doing this can make it seem as if a believer has to be committed to belief in a logical, formal contradiction. Kierkegaard does not, however, mean that the believer is so committed. Instead of making Climacus develop an argument to show that the statements 'God is eternal' and 'God became man' are consistent statements, as many great theologians have done,[16] Climacus is made to do the opposite, to press the presentation of doctrine as contradiction. By so doing he indicates the limitation of human reason and shows the presumptuousness of humans asserting knowledge of eternity; he also drives the believer away from a purely intellectual preoccupation with Christianity through burdening the intellect with impossibility almost in the style of the Zen koan.[17] Thus one must not take Climacus' statements to mean that Kierkegaard is an irrationalist. The claims go against reason because they go against particular finite human assumptions about the nature of God and the universe.[18]

While the intense Christian life-style presented by Climacus in *Philosophical Fragments* and *Concluding Unscientific Postscript* need not come in conflict with the culture, insofar as the type of spirituality presented is still intellectually the presuppositions of a Christian culture, one can see that it is likely to come in conflict with any Christian culture that shares Judge William's outlook. Even though Judge William leaves room for individual development in the personal God-relationship, it is inescapable that self-renunciation of the kind depicted in the Climacus writings is at best in some tension with community Christianity. The struggle to arrive at detachment from partiality in personal relationships to family, friends and race, illustrates this, as does the factor of readiness to give up everything for the sake of the God-relationship. Also, as we have seen, a religiosity that has place for the renunciation of marriage (or any partnerships that have place for the begetting of children) assumes, as part of its ethical-religious ideal, renunciation of the physical presupposition for the very existence of any community. Seen from this perspective, although on the one hand Christianity strengthens the life of community in working against personal selfishness – and, since it is intrinsically bound up with ethics, in insisting on fulfilment of the ethical-religious ideal in its 'you shall love' – Christianity in its ideality must be seen as an 'asocial' principle.[19] There is movement from a mild altruism to an intensive altruism in which others are viewed as part of the area of one's selfhood, and thus to be renounced or given up if God calls upon one to do so.

Secondly, Christianity may be acceptable insofar as it is not anti-social in the sense of directly destructive of community life, but still cause conflict insofar as its intellectual presuppositions conflict with the community's overall world-picture. Even in a pluralistic world, scientific theories about existence and the universe may be accepted currently that conflict with Christian assumptions. As especially Climacus shows in his presentation of the intellectual aspect of Christianity, Christianity can conflict with philosophical, religious and cultural assumptions about the nature of existence where accounts of the life and work of Jesus are concerned. Even in societies where a religious perspective is dominant, claims about the figure of Jesus can be a source of conflict.[20]

Thirdly, Christianity may find itself in a situation of acute conflict if it is practised in a culture that views its life-style as a threat to society. The early Roman Empire and former Soviet Russia are examples that spring to mind, while the history of the Evangelical Christian Lutheran Church in Tanzania is an interesting example of a modern group that started out as a persecuted minority but came to be accepted by the wider community. In cases where the adherents of Christianity do come to be so accepted, the nature of, and reasons for, the acceptance may be many and varied. The wider community might come to agree with the assumptions belonging to Christian doctrine and practice. The wider community might base its main world-view on something non-religious – for example, the findings of science – and tolerate a plurality of religious groups. The Christian congregation might compromise the Christian message slightly in order to secure religious toleration, or, if the entire society regarded itself as Christian, it might retain the Christian label but gradually slip into the philistinism condemned by Kierkegaard.

Where the possibility of martyrdom is concerned, Kierkegaard considers that although serious imitation of Christ will provoke hostile reaction that becomes a lifelong martyrdom of suffering, the Christian should not seek physical martyrdom.[21] To seek martyrdom can be a form of self-love that does not mind causing the enemy to be guilty of one's death and also assumes that one definitely possesses the truth. A Christian should, however, be ready to suffer martyrdom if called upon to do so, and martyrdom has value in itself seen as an ultimate form of self-renunciation. It must, though, be undertaken with the emphasis on holding fast to living Christianly.[22] Seen from a human perspective, Christ's life was asocial in its obedience to God because he was the pattern of the self-renunciation that included giving up family, marriage and life. Jesus is thus the pattern of religious ideality within the ethical-religious as part of the individual's forward striving to do the good and the right. Such a pattern lies ultimately beyond the ordinary universal ethical, which latter, in the light of such ultimate ideality, appears as a 'higher egoism' for controlling personal egoisms through law. Extreme imitators of Christ can therefore expect negative reaction from those within a Christian community[23] as well as from those outside it.

DIVINE COMMAND AND REVELATION

As we have seen above, the attitude of 'resignation', in which the individual is ready to give up the good things of temporality for God, can be innocuous in relation to the community (Christian or otherwise), since one can give up a number of temporal goods and relationships without concretely conflicting with society. When in *Fear and Trembling*, Kierkegaard's pseudonym describes the movements of resignation and faith using the story of a man who gives up his princess (Kierkegaard and Regine), and the man who does this yet believes at the same time that he will get her back, the activity of the man posits no threat to the community.[24] Resignation is, however, a negative action to the extent that it does not involve concrete action in relation to others; and similarly, any form of faith against the understanding that stops with intellectual commitment to propositions (the restoration of the princess, that Jesus is God incarnate), or confines its activity to loving, totally altruistic service to the community for the sake of the propositions, is, from a practical viewpoint, harmless to the community, where it is not positively constructive.

As Kierkegaard clearly sees, however, problems can arise as soon as one posits a view of the universe in which God reveals himself to the world from a position above and beyond society,[25] or, concerning self-renunciation, one views one's area of selfhood as larger than one's personal identity and comes to involve others in one's actions. Where God is thus viewed as above and beyond the sphere of the community or 'universal', it is only the goodness of God that guarantees the ethical and the ethical-religious distinction between right and wrong. To put it another way, if God is not intrinsically good, thus always requiring *moral* action, then whatever God is seen as requiring takes precedence, whatever it is. Where, however, 'the ethical as such is the universal', the moral code is moral insofar as its principles genuinely apply to all. That is, community needs and values play a part in what is to be defined as good behaviour.[26] Where God is viewed as above and beyond the sphere of community, difficulties begin as soon as the divinity is the source of requirements and/or messages that conflict with the community's daily ethical code, whether it be the code of a primitive tribe or the content of Balle's catechism.

To illustrate this, it is useful to consider different types of divinely revealed command to individuals, taking for granted that the individual concerned genuinely wishes to do the right thing. A good example of a mild type is the foundation of the Salesian Order by St John Bosco. Inspired by visionary dreams, John Bosco battled against all difficulties, including the opposition of superiors, to carry out his mission to children.[27] Here, the actual requirement was to do practical good in the community, and the (temporary) conflict was purely with those lacking the breadth of gospel vision in its social application. Bosco's self-renunciation was in relation to his calling as a Roman Catholic priest and the needs of his mission. One can label the inspiration of Bosco's mission as a private communication or inspiration to him from God to carry out an ethical task for the community.

If we look at the story of Abraham discussed in Kierkegaard's *Fear and Trembling*, the situation is very different. Again we have a private divine communication to an individual, but here, there is nothing to be done for the community. Abraham is called upon to make a great act of self-renunciation in sacrificing his only son to God. We can note that Abraham is asked to do something devastating. In viewing Isaac as part of his area of selfhood to be sacrificed, he is going further than the potential sacrifice of his son, he is to wipe out all prospect of the nation he is to found. In other words, he is called upon to sacrifice the potentiality of an entire community. Furthermore, he cannot justify his action by appealing to a higher community good or value within society, nor can he even appeal to God's previous communications, since these have all had to do with how he is to have a son and found a new nation. No community good is served by the potential sacrifice (that flagrantly ignores Isaac's value as an individual in his own right and the duty of parent to care for child). The only good in the affair is Abraham's continuity of desire to do the right thing, and since he is sure God has commanded it, he has faith that he is doing that. That he is justified by the result, that it turns out to have been God's test of his self-renouncing love, that the ram turns up at the last moment, is beside the point. As also Aldous Huxley points out,[28] the question is how the individual, however pious, is to distinguish between the prompting of the Holy Spirit and the prompting of the spirit of craziness. Kierkegaard answers this question to a certain extent in his analysis of the case of Pastor Adolph Adler, who claimed in 1842 that he had received a personal revelation from Jesus.[29] In 1846, Kierkegaard, who had written his analysis of the sacrifice of Isaac, also his criticisms of objectively certain truth in the Climacus writings, felt compelled to examine the case of Pastor Adler on the basis of Adler's own claims.[30] Kierkegaard initially had argued that concerning claims made by Jesus, the individual must choose the attitude of offence or faith. In the case of Adler, however, he perceived that in such cases, one should look at the circumstances surrounding the claims made, before making one's decision.

In his unpublished *The Book on Adler*, Kierkegaard arrives at four criteria one could apply in such a situation. The first is whether there is any incoherence or confusion surrounding the alleged instance of personal revelation. Kierkegaard found such incoherence in the writings of Adler, where the text is sometimes so confused as to be unreadable. In a personal interview Kierkegaard was also struck by Adler's assumption that Kierkegaard would understand the alleged revelation for himself if Adler read it to him in a whispering voice.[31] The second criterion is whether the 'revelation' really brings anything new when one compares its content with the presuppositions of the established order. If, as in Adler's case, there is nothing new, one can hardly speak of a revelation of the unknown. Thirdly, Kierkegaard looks for consistency of claim concerning the nature of the event. While it is perfectly in order for an individual to change the claim, revoking a previous one, it is unacceptable for that person to make several totally different and conflicting claims about the same event without revoking any of them. Finally, and importantly, the individual must self-evidently be a mature and godly person in every sense of the word.

Kierkegaard found that Adler failed all four criteria and was clearly in a state of mental confusion. The criteria emerge from Kierkegaard's investigation of the case, and it is commendable that he examined the affair on the basis of Adler's own premises instead of dismissing the pastor in advance as heretical and crazy. Kierkegaard is not here intending to present us with some cut-and-dried method for deciding about personal divine commands and messages, but his criteria may well be helpful in assessing situations such as that of Pastor Jim Jones in Guyana or the Branch Davidians in Texas.[32] It is not entirely clear, however, how far they help in the situation where the person is or becomes the message – acts as a Messiah who wishes to introduce the community to a new way of life and does it with a measure of consistency.

Claims to be a, or the, Messiah were plentiful in Jesus' time and are today, as are claims to be a divinely sponsored leader.[33] In such cases, however much the leader may urge reformation or fulfilment of the present religion of the community, the new movement usually comes in conflict with the religious establishment and risks persecution if it cannot gain a firm foothold and perhaps even become the new establishment. In such cases there is the possibility that a strong personality will sway the masses and overthrow the established order.[34] In *The Book on Adler* Kierkegaard seems to find his fourth criterion about godliness of life to be outstandingly important, so much so, that he uses it as a test of the founder of Christianity when he says:

> If Christ had not triumphed through being crucified, but had triumphed in the modern style through officiousness and a frightful use of the gab, so that no voter could refuse him a vote, if he had triumphed through a craftiness that could make people believe anything, if Christianity had come into the world victorious in that manner and Christ had been regarded as God's Son, then it was certainly not Christianity that had come and Christ would definitely not have been God's Son. What had triumphed would have been not Christianity, but a parody of it.[35]

For Kierkegaard, the authentic religious leader, whatever the precise nature of the claim, is godlike through being Christlike. Such a person is not self-assertive, bragging and egoistic, but an authentically humble figure whose strength is the strength of a genuinely godly character.

Thus far, good. Kierkegaard's criterion certainly seems to weed out money-making television Messiahs and potential Hitlers. It may even allow for the humble leader who radiates saintliness but is philosophically confused in his or her concepts (and thus perhaps falls foul of the second and third criteria). What it cannot do is to remove the need for choice of faith or offence. Kierkegaard tests Christianity by the figure of Christ, but the figure of Christ, coming as it does from Christianity, cannot, as he realizes, be an ultimate test of itself but only an accepted test of the validity of forms of Christianity or religiosity. Apart from this, the only other criterion is the application of general duties to be found in every culture. These can be summed up as follows: helping others and not harming them, duties to kin and posterity, the laws of truthfulness, justice and mercy.[36] These would, though, still only validate the ethical-religious life in its universal community expression. They would not help in extreme Abraham–Isaac situations or guide an individual in his or her God-relationship, if that individual were considering a call to give up everything for a more intense spiritual life than one in the ordinary temporal community.

It is at this point that Kierkegaard leaves room for divine activity. In *The Book on Adler*, he speaks of apostolic authority as stemming from the sphere of transcendence or eternity.[37] In *Philosophical Fragments* the initiative is clearly with Jesus as the God-Man, and for the same reason. The factor of divine initiative is so strong for Kierkegaard that he lets Climacus state that it would be sufficient for the modern prospective believer if the contemporaries of Jesus had left nothing behind except the words: 'We have believed that in such and such a year the god appeared in the humble form of a servant, lived and taught among us, and then died.'[38] At first sight, this strikes the reader as absurd, since the words say absolutely nothing to a person who has never heard of Christianity. It also leaps over the question of whether Jesus ever did claim to be God. Despite the importance of Kierkegaard's arguments about the insecurity of objective historical knowledge, in *Concluding Unscientific Postscript*, there is a difference between a report of someone's Messianic or divine claims and actually experiencing them for oneself. With the former, there is always a chance that the person has been misunderstood or misrepresented. Yet the point at issue is still one of personal commitment. Given the truth of Kierkegaard's assumption that there is a God, that there is a real eternal sphere of existence beyond the temporal world, the vital element of the individual's spiritual existence will be the initial commitment to the God-relationship. A person might even disbelieve much of the intellectual content of Christianity, for example, the Virgin birth, that Christ was God incarnate, but still venture to try living within the ethical-religious requirements of Christianity and experience a real encounter with God.[39] Just as Judge William's advice to the aesthete is the occasion for the latter to encounter God in the ethical life, so does whatever starts a person off on the Christian life act as a trigger or an occasion. Kierkegaard (like Judge William as well as Socrates[40]) himself aims to act as such an occasion and is surely right to see the doctrinal content as of less significance than the existential life-style given that Christianity is a way of life. Yet if he stresses doctrinal uncertainty and offence, he encourages the believer to be on the watch against bogus religiosity wherever and however this manifests itself.

Notes

1. PAP, XI,2 A 153; XI,1 A 190; cf. SV, VI, pp. 98, 161 (SLW); SV, II, pp. 223–4 (EOII).
2. As Kierkegaard points out, SV, XIII, pp. 359–60 (CI). In *Works of Love*, SV, IX, p. 55 (WL), 'the flesh' is understood to be 'selfishness'. In the journals of the final years he associates the idea of the fall into sin with human propagation divorced from the ideality of spiritual existence: PAP, XI,2 A 201, cf. 150 (JP).
3. SV, II, p. 57 (EOII).
4. Anti-Climacus thinks God will let each person know what is required, and Kierkegaard allows for both the monastery and marriage as forms of total renunciation. See SV, XII, p. 64 (PC); PAP, VIII,1 A 403; XI,1 A 134; XI,2 A 301 (JP).
5. SV, VII, p. 498 (CUP).
6. SV, IX, pp. 47–62, 135 (WL); cf. SV, VII, pp. 428, 403, 335–6, 341–2 (CUP).
7. A good example of this is Jean Vianney, curé of Ars in France, who regarded his enormous work as nothing and himself as the worst of sinners.
8. SV, VII, pp. 458–84, 174 (CUP).
9. This is what Climacus means when he speaks of 'every remnant of original immanence' being annihilated. The 'connection' that is cut away (SV, VII, pp. 498–9) is the potentiality of the eternal in the self through the development of which, in ethical-religious striving, the individual could achieve his or her own eternal bliss.
10. Two works to be commended especially here are C. Stephen Evans, *Passionate Reason: Making Sense of Kierkegaard's 'Philosophical Fragments'* and C. Stephen Evans, *Kierkegaard's 'Fragments' and 'Postscript': The Religious Philosophy of Johannes Climacus* (Atlantic Highlands, NJ: Humanities Press, 1983).
11. SV, VII, pp. 128–31 (CUP); cf. Peter Atkins, *Creation Revisited* (London: Penguin Books, 1992), pp. vii, 107, who asserts that 'the human brain is an instrument of limitless power' and believes that we can arrive at 'a theory of everything' in the universe.
12. See here especially SV, VII, Part One (CUP).
13. As Kierkegaard-Climacus points out (SV, IV, pp. 244–5 (PF)), if I look at a star in the night sky I am conscious of a twinkling spark of light, but the cosmologist's information about the star's origin is object of my belief, not something I know for certain.
14. SV, IV, pp. 211–12, 231 (PF); SV, VII, pp. 166, 169–79, 492, 168, 189–90, 196, 372–3, 495, 183–4 (CUP); PAP, XI,2 A 301 (JP).
15. SV, IV, pp. 255–6, 221–34, 252–71 (PF); SV, VII, p. 486 (CUP). On offence and the distinction between sacred and profane history, see also SV, XII, e.g. pp. 24, 113–14 (PC).

16. For a twentieth-century attempt, see F. C. Happold, *Religious Faith and Twentieth-Century Man* (Harmondsworth: Penguin Books, 1966), pp. 134–57.
17. One can also compare here the movement away from conceptualization of God in *The Cloud of Unknowing*: Clifton Wolters (tr.), *The Cloud of Unknowing and Other Works* (Harmondsworth: Penguin Books, 1961, 1978), pp. 67–8.
18. See here Stephen Evans' arguments in *Passionate Reason*, pp. 96–118, and in *Kierkegaard's 'Fragments'*, pp. 207–80.
19. PAP, XI,1 A 190 (JP).
20. This may be true even where religions include similar ideas, e.g. the notion of divine grace to be found in the Shinran sect of the Pure Land Buddhism, if Christians view Jesus as exclusively bringer of grace, while the history of denominational in-fighting demonstrates that difficulties can arise between even Christian groups.
21. PAP, IX A 325 (JP); Kierkegaard, 'Has a man the right to let himself be put to death for the truth?', SV, XI, pp. 55–91 (PA, pp. 77–135).
22. PAP, X,3 A 498, 303; XI,1 A 462 (JP).
23. Kierkegaard's ambiguous attitude to Bishop Mynster, who is paradigm and yet to be attacked (see Chapter 3), can be seen in the light of the tension between Christianity lived as community ethics and Christianity in its ideality of self-renunciation. On the State as a higher egoism, see PAP, XI,2 A 108, 111 (JP).
24. SV, III, pp. 85–100 (FT/R). On *Fear and Trembling*, see Robert L. Perkins (ed.), *Kierkegaard's 'Fear and Trembling': Critical Appraisals* (Alabama: The University of Alabama Press, 1981); Robert L. Perkins (ed.), *International Kierkegaard Commentary: 'Fear and Trembling'* (Macon, GA: Mercer University Press, 1993); Edward F. Mooney, *Knights of Faith and Resignation: Reading Kierkegaard's 'Fear and Trembling'* (Albany, NY: State University of New York Press, 1991).
25. In Kierkegaard's writings, e.g. in *Fear and Trembling* and *Concluding Unscientific Postscript*, Hegel's God is within the world-historical process and revelation unfolds from within the process.
26. Johannes de silentio is thus correct to complain (SV, III, pp. 82, 104–5 (FT/R)) that, on the Hegelian view that 'the ethical is the universal', Abraham is a potential murderer.
27. Henri Ghéon, *The Secret of Saint John Bosco* (London: Sheed & Ward, 1935).
28. Aldous Huxley (citing Bayle), *The Devils of Loudun* (New York: Carroll & Graf Publishers, Inc., 1986), p. 86. The story Huxley alludes to is that of a pious young Anabaptist who thought God had commanded him to sacrifice his brother and carried it out (with the brother's full assent).
29. It should be noted that Adler's case essentially concerned possible conflict with Christian doctrine, not with the ethical content of Christianity.
30. PAP, VII,2 B 235 (OAR).
31. On the Adler affair, see Julia Watkin, 'The criteria of ethical-religious authority: Kierkegaard and Adolph Adler', *ACME – Annali della*

Facoltà di Lettere e Filosofia dell'Università degli Studi di Milano 45.1 (January–April 1992), pp. 27–40.

32. On Pastor Jim Jones see *Time*, 'Cult of death', 4 December 1978, pp. 6–14. On Branch Davidians, see *Time*, 'Tragedy in Waco', 3 May 1993, pp. 26–43; *Newsweek*, 'Last days of the Waco cult – death wish', 3 May 1993, pp. 10–17.

33. See for example Pastor Sun Myung Moon's divine call to be a religious leader and 'establish the Kingdom of Heaven on the earth': John Biermans, Michael Giampaoli and others, 'Profile of Rev. Moon's life', *New Vision for World Peace* (Chung H. Kwak, Holy Spirit Association for the Unification of World Christianity, 1988), p. 58.

34. Such 'Messianic' movements may operate in a more secular manner, where a person claims to be God's divine instrument for political change. This was the case with Hitler, judging from some of his speeches (German television series, *Hitler – A Profile*, Guido Knopp, Ivan Fila, Nina Steinhauser, and others, ZDF/SBS, 1996).

35. PAP, VII,2 B 235, fn. p. 51 (OAR, ft. pp. 42–3).

36. C. S. Lewis gathers a list together from classical, Christian and oriental thought, though only as testimony for a natural law ethic, and not in proof of it: C. S. Lewis, *The Abolition of Man* (London and Glasgow: Collins Fount Paperbacks, 1984).

37. PAP, VII,2 B 235, pp. 143–6 (OAR, pp. 110–12).

38. SV, IV, p. 266 (PF). Climacus calls this a 'world-historical *nota bene*'.

39. Even where an individual does not believe in anything beyond the present world, or assuming that there was nothing beyond the world, there would, of course, be the possibility of ethical, or some form of ethical-religious, development.

40. Judge William suggests that the young aesthete should throw away the rest of his letter if he has understood what he means and is ready to commit himself to living ethically: SV, II, p. 152 (EOII).

7

Kierkegaard and the Christian tradition

We have yet to consider Kierkegaard's relation to the wider Christian tradition in which he was situated and the phenomenon of his great influence on Christian thinkers after him. In what follows I will first endeavour to indicate briefly how he related to the Christian tradition and then show why he has been hailed as one of the makers of the modern theological mind. When, however, one seeks to show Kierkegaard's significance in relation to figures in the Christian tradition before him, one has to face at the outset the difficulty presented by his manner of working. While he can be placed firmly within the Protestant Lutheran tradition, he constantly breaks out of it in order to deal with the problems he saw authentic Christianity facing in nineteenth-century Denmark; and he breaks out of it in an unsystematic way, even though, of course, he had received a thorough grounding in theology at the university.

As Johannes Sløk points out,[1] it was exceedingly difficult for Kierkegaard to concern himself objectively with another author, and hence he often not only deals with Christian theologians unsystematically, he also often utilizes incidental elements of their positions that he happens to encounter in his reading. In relating them to points he wishes to make in his own writing, he is, however, not afraid to be critical of such theologians or to deal with difficulties in their presentation of Christian doctrine, even when he is not thoroughly versed in the main corpus of their writings. Nor does he find it in any way contradictory to read theologians' works for devotional purposes and yet be critical of aspects of their theology. The strength of this approach is that he does not let

94

himself be bound narrowly to a particular strand of theological orthodoxy, but freely uses the entire Christian tradition accessible to him for his Socratic preaching of Christianity. This can be seen not only from the allusions to Catholic as well as Protestant writers in his authorship; it can also be seen from the number of books by Catholic authors, dealing with Catholic themes, that still remained in Kierkegaard's library at his death.[2] The weakness or difficulty of this approach is that one cannot expect from Kierkegaard an in-depth discussion of the total views of such theologians. He rather assesses and grasps the far-reaching implications of what he encounters, and does it, albeit brilliantly, through a sometimes one-sided perspective.

Kierkegaard's method of working is illustrated especially by his attitude to Luther, where on the one hand he maintains the Lutheran emphasis on free forgiveness of sins through the grace of God in Christ, but on the other is compelled by the misuse of grace in Danish Christendom to act as a corrective to the Lutheran corrective and assert the rigour of the Law.[3] In this way, Kierkegaard reasserts the spirit of Luther even in his attack on the abuse of Luther's position and in his criticism of him.[4] Similarly, one can note Kierkegaard's critical support of Augustine's view of fall doctrine and hereditary sin. Kierkegaard stands against Pelagius' optimistic view of sin and humankind, seeing it as an earlier version of the contemporary effort to make Christianity fit agreeably into the world. Thus Kierkegaard supports the Augustinian view of human fallenness against Pelagius but later accuses Augustine of conceptualizing Christianity, of having confused the concept of faith by turning faith as a personal God-relationship into belief in intellectual propositions.[5]

Criticism of Augustine's view of sin emerges particularly in Kierkegaard's psychological investigation of the experience of sin in *The Concept of Anxiety*. Here, the problems of Augustine's presentation of fall doctrine emerge clearly in Vigilius Haufniensis' criticism of traditional concepts of hereditary sin. If one starts with a view of Adam as initially a perfect superman figure outside the race and describes hereditary sin introduced at the fall as if it were a continuing genetic taint, one also involving legal culpability, there is firstly a problem concerning Adam's status as genuinely representative of the human race. Secondly, it is hard to retain the idea of human freedom in the face of the implication that one is responsible for what one cannot really help. Kierkegaard deals with the problems by including Adam as an ordinary human in the race: for Adam, as well as for every human, 'sin comes into the world by a sin'. Every individual is free not to sin and sins in freedom, not of necessity. Yet each individual is also a member of the human race. Once the phenomenon of sin has occurred there is a (growing) burden of sin in the human race as its history progresses. This burden expresses itself in the accumulation of the consequences of human sins and through the knowledge of what sin is, which knowledge presents itself to the individual in the psychological attraction–repulsion situation of the anxiety experience and also in the moral taking of responsibility for human sinfulness.[6] Kierkegaard thus aligns himself with Augustine and other Christian thinkers in accepting the main outline of the doctrine of fall and hereditary sin, but shifts it away from dogmatics into the sphere of psychological and moral experience. In the process he attempts to eliminate what he sees as absurdities resulting from such a conceptual treatment of the Christian doctrine.[7]

Finally, Kierkegaard's freedom in his use of the Christian tradition can be seen in relation to Pietism and Lutheranism as he encountered them in Denmark. Here again we see a critical application of elements of both traditions as he understands these to conform to the teachings of the New Testament, to agree with the Christian's religious experience, and to assist his task as a religious writer in 'Christendom'. As Marie Thulstrup points out,[8] Kierkegaard's attitude to Pietism was not uncritical. As it tended to present Christianity as personal morality in relation to a collection of rules and prohibitions, Kierkegaard rejected it; as it emphasized the positive value of suffering arising from self-denial and persecution by the world, he came to hail it as 'the one and only consequence of Christianity'.[9] Like the Pietists, Kierkegaard polemicized against personal justification by faith alone, conceived purely intellectually without the response of works, and like the Pietists he sought, not reform, but understanding and application of Christian doctrine in personal realization of it.[10] Christianity called for conversion and dying to the world, in the light of the primeval fall into sin, redemption through Christ and the acknowledgement of a gradual degeneration of the Christian Church since the time of the Apostles. Whereas the Pietists stressed the need of conversion and a successful programme of personal holiness for all Christians, however, Kierkegaard came, in the context of the attack on 'Christendom', to emphasize the primitive Christian experience of sacrifice and martyrdom. The final section of Kierkegaard's journals are thus filled with references to the Apostles, to the Church Fathers, and to spiritual figures in the Christian tradition as Kierkegaard moves from the emphasis on conversion and inward imitation of Christ to emphasis on the outer signs of persecution and martyrdom.[11]

For Balle's catechism and Mynster, conversion is not the once-only sudden beginning of the path to holiness, but a daily process fulfilling Luther's description of the individual as *simul justus et peccator*, at the same time justified and sinner. Conversion never leads to more than a new conversion, with fulfilment beyond the grave. In Kierkegaard, conversion is a once-only radical occurrence, and the 'true Christian' must be one who has progressed from that experience by imitation of Christ, self-denial and dying to the world.[12] Unlike the Pietists, however, Kierkegaard's 'progress' works, as we have seen, on the principle of the more real progress, the greater the real discovery of sin, so that however much the progress, it can never in practice lead to fulfilment in this life or to reliance on 'works'. In this way, through his analysis of the individual's actual experience, he retains the sense of continualness in Balle and Mynster concerning sin and repentance, but it is separated from the basic conversion experience and has a depth of psychological profundity lacking in both.

We can thus see in Kierkegaard's use of the Christian tradition a continuous attempt to demonstrate Christian doctrine in concrete existential terms, emphasizing precisely those doctrines, or elements of those doctrines, that can act as the needed corrective in the contemporary religious situation. Yet at the same time he was not afraid to tackle head-on difficulties he found in the doctrinal concepts presented in the history of the Church. Given that Kierkegaard drew as widely and as freely as he did on the entire Christian tradition, it is not surprising that his writings have influenced theologians and thinkers from a wide range of Christian standpoints. This, combined with what Louis Dupré has described as Kierkegaard's unshaken faithfulness to the Protestant principle and his ability to show that some theological problems were really fictitious, enabled Kierkegaard to adopt an approach to Catholicism and Protestantism that enabled many coming under his influence to become committed Catholics and Protestants.[13] What we now need to consider, however, is why he has been hailed as one of the makers of the modern theological mind.

Initially, apart from having some immediate influence in Denmark after his death,[14] Kierkegaard seemed fated to be disregarded. If we set aside the problem that he wrote in Danish rather than in a major language, it can be seen that Kierkegaard was out of step with current trends in theology – with the approach to truth through the historical process and developing Pietist interest in social and political concerns. Until the beginning of the twentieth century Kierkegaard was practically unknown outside Scandinavia, while he was ignored by nineteenth-century Liberal Protestantism.[15] Yet, with two world wars and the decline of optimism concerning human progress, Kierkegaard's thought made its delayed impact in our century. Crisis theologian Emil Brunner calls him 'the greatest Christian thinker of modern time'.[16] He is 'one of the most important, if not the most important, figure in the philosophy and theology of our time' (Paul Roubiczek),[17] 'one of the first "modern" thinkers – the first who made a decisive break with a long-established philosophical tradition in order to portray the human condition in the light of hitherto unsuspected or neglected existential possibilities' (Ronald Grimsley).[18]

In looking at Kierkegaard's influence on modern theology, we need to remember that some of Kierkegaard's theological influence was mediated through the philosophical element of his thought and through thinkers who were not theologians. Great care therefore needs to be taken not to draw up fixed 'philosophical' and 'theological' demarcation lines of historical development. Nor should the word 'influence' be used of Kierkegaard's relation to figures coming after him, if this is meant to indicate that Kierkegaard has left some uniform manner of thinking in his wake. Apart from the fact that parallels between thinkers do not necessarily indicate influence, even where one thinker has read another, to use the word in the sense of straight appropriation of ideas is totally inadequate where the later thinker has taken up and emphasized one or two elements of his source in a very different direction. Thus great care is needed in speaking of e.g. Kierkegaard's influence on Jean-Paul Sartre,[19] in whom (if one is searching for parallels) Kierkegaard's emphasis on existence, freedom and choice can be found, but magnified and taken in a different and atheistic direction that Kierkegaard would have rejected.[20] If one bears this reservation in mind, however, and takes 'influence' to mean stimulus to creative thinking, Kierkegaard can be spoken of as a source of inspiration behind the movement known as 'existentialism', where his writings have been a liberating inspiration in various degrees to thinkers such as Martin Heidegger (1889–1976) and Karl Jaspers (1883–1969). One can note Jaspers' mixed reaction to Kierkegaard when he says:

I adopted his [Kierkegaard's] 'concept' of Existence. But I did not become his disciple. His Christianity left me untouched, and in his negative choices – no marriage, no office, no realization in the world; instead a martyr's existence as essential to Christian truth – I sensed the very opposite of everything I loved and wanted, of everything I was willing or unwilling to do. Both this practical negativism and his 'religiousness B' with its view of Christian faith as absurd seemed to me the end of historic Christianity as well as the end of philosophical life. It was the more astonishing, all but inexhaustibly stimulating, what Kierkegaard in his honesty managed to see and to say by the way. Today, I felt, there could be no philosophy without him.[21]

The phenomenon of mixed reaction is perhaps best manifested in the work of the famous Protestant theologian Karl Barth (1886–1968), who was one of the first major Christian theologians to draw inspiration from Kierkegaard's writings. In the 1921 second edition of his commentary, *The Epistle to the Romans*, Barth (who first encountered Kierkegaard in 1909 in a German translation of Kierkegaard's *The Instant*) acknowledges his debt to Kierkegaard and places him among the really great ones: Abraham, Jeremiah, Socrates, Grünewald, Luther and Dostoevsky. In a lecture from the following year, 1922, Kierkegaard appears in a list of Barth's spiritual ancestors, of whom the others are Luther, Calvin, St Paul and Jeremiah.

Barth emphasizes the Kierkegaardian infinite qualitative distinction between time and eternity, the gap between God and humans, though, as N. H. Søe points out in an article on Kierkegaard and Barth,[22] Kierkegaard was not the only source of this important theme in Barth, while even in Barth's severe judgement of human existence there is a difference between him and Kierkegaard in that Kierkegaard attacks the phenomenon of a debased 'Christendom', whereas Barth seems to pronounce a judgement on earthly existence. Yet Barth agrees with Kierkegaard in emphasizing the Lutheran *theologia crucis*, theology of the cross, as opposed to the *theologia gloriae*, theology of glory, and like Kierkegaard he underlines the thought that God cannot be directly recognized. As with Kierkegaard, Barth's Christ is the lowly servant, source of 'offence', and the human spiritual condition is one of struggle and forsakenness rather than peace. For both, the non-believer's situation is one of despair. Also in Barth is to be found faith as miracle and paradox, though Barth's interest is theological whereas Kierkegaard emphasizes the psychology of faith.

On the publication of his *Christian Dogmatics* in 1927, Barth still mentions Kierkegaard, together with nine other theologians to whom he is greatly indebted. Yet after this Kierkegaard disappears more and more, and when he is mentioned, it is with criticism. Now it is true that the early Barth found points of disagreement with Kierkegaard – in his commentary on Romans he was critical of what he saw as Kierkegaard's excessive pietism and of his 'teleological suspension of the ethical' – but there is clearly a serious turning away from Kierkegaard in the later Barth. In his Sonning Prize speech on 19 April 1963, at the University of Copenhagen,[23] Barth states his later disagreement clearly. He says that in his youth he was captivated by Kierkegaard's emphasis on taking the gospel's absolute requirement seriously and personally, finding it an antidote to the Liberal Protestant union of culture and Christianity. Yet he gradually found Kierkegaard's incessant proclamation of the practice of Christianity a threat to the gospel of God's free grace. Secondly, he came to feel that Kierkegaard's focus on the individual was to the detriment of congregation and Church community, of Church missionary work and its social and political tasks. Finally, Barth says the notion that subjectivity is truth made the sequel of an existential philosophy reasonable, for the emphasis on subjectivity can lead to a faith that finds its foundation in itself and becomes, in the mid-twentieth century, groundless and objectless. Far from attacking the anthropocentric-Christian line of thinking of the time, Kierkegaard had in fact greatly strengthened it. Barth concludes:

> In the light of these later insights, I am, and remain, thankful as before to Kierkegaard for the immunization he gave me in those days. I am, and remain, filled with deep respect for the genuinely tragic nature of his life and for the extraordinary lustre of his works. I consider him to be a teacher into whose school every theologian must go once. Woe to him who has missed it! So long as he does not remain in or return to it! His teaching is, as he himself once put it, a 'touch of spice' for the food, not the food itself, which it is the task of right theology to offer to the church and thus to men. The Gospel is firstly the glad news of God's Yes to man. It is secondly the news which the congregation must pass on to the whole world. It is thirdly the news from on high. These are the three aspects in relation to which I had to do

further study – after my meeting Kierkegaard – in the school of other teachers.

In his article, Søe does not attempt to answer Barth's criticisms, but a brief general answer to them may help to show how Kierkegaard is able to be a source of inspiration to a wide range of divergent thinkers. In short, one can say that Barth missed the scope of the Socratic element of Kierkegaard's form of communication that enabled Kierkegaard to discuss with the reader a variety of different life-styles and perspectives; he also seems to have missed the sense of balance which made Kierkegaard stress that his theological emphasis was a needed corrective, but one that should not be used without further ado as a norm for another generation in a different situation.[24] In Kierkegaard, emphasis on the individual is balanced by his positive approach to the creation of community (through the initial reform of the individual) in *Works of Love*,[25] and his emphasis on subjectivity is balanced by his realistic grasp of the questions surrounding the individual's faith-relation to the objective content of Christianity. One result of Kierkegaard's approach was that a number of divergent thinkers could find in him a source of inspiration in relation to their contemporary situations. This explains why three other important theologians, Rudolf Bultmann (1884–1976), Paul Tillich (1886–1965) and Dietrich Bonhoeffer (1906–45), could draw upon Kierkegaard's insights.[26]

Bultmann's inspiration by Kierkegaard chiefly concerns Kierkegaard's presentation of revelation, though this does not mean that he bases his theology on Kierkegaard texts. Bultmann took over certain basic structures in Kierkegaard's thought, but often through Barth, and to some extent perhaps through Heidegger, though, as Jørgen K. Bukdahl points out,[27] Kierkegaard probably already influenced Bultmann's reading and interpretation of Heidegger. Bultmann's elaboration of Kierkegaard themes is, however, creatively independent. He cites Kierkegaard when he wishes to refute theologians whom he sees as unjustifiably claiming Kierkegaard's support, but where he appears to have been influenced by Kierkegaard he rarely mentions him. He seems to take over Kierkegaard perspectives in a direct interpretation of primitive Christianity. Parallels with Kierkegaard can be found in Bultmann's concept of revelation, in the distinction between thought and actuality, in Bultmann's view of the historic character of human life and the problem of approximation to objective truth.

Paul Tillich encountered Kierkegaard twice. As a young theology student at Halle, Tillich read translations of Kierkegaard. 'In the years 1905–1907', he says later, 'we were grasped by Kierkegaard. It was a great experience.'[28] The young Tillich was struck by the 'intense piety' in Kierkegaard that went to the heart of human existence, but it was the post-First-World-War Tillich on whom the work of Heidegger, Kierkegaard, and Kierkegaard through Barth, made a real impact. In Tillich's thought, one can see Kierkegaard's analysis of the human situation, and his treatment of human freedom, choice and faith shows the inspiration of Kierkegaard, whom Tillich names, among many other references to him, in relation to the Tillichean theme of 'ultimate concern'.[29] Like Kierkegaard, Tillich emphasizes the gulf between God and humankind, the need of divine revelation and the inevitability of the language of paradox to express it, but he is not afraid to explore the metaphysics or ontological structure of theology. Tillich's 'method of correlation', which Tillich sees as his task especially in his *Systematic Theology*, arises from his belief that theology (the gospel) must answer philosophy's questions about existence, as for instance when the sense of human estrangement receives its response in the New Being in Christ. With his use of the idea of God as 'the ground of being' who manifests himself in a revelatory experience, Tillich especially targets the attempt in Christian theology to turn God into some kind of entity. Here, Tillich clearly follows Kierkegaard's rejection of the attempt to turn God into a finite idol, but he seeks to retain the mystical element of religion using language he feels appropriate to the twentieth century.

Bonhoeffer's concern about how to translate the gospel into modern terms was linked to his assumption that Western culture was moving towards a post-Christian era. He did not see that Barth's biblicism of the Holy Spirit or the existentialism of Bultmann and Tillich could provide an answer. Instead, Bonhoeffer urges that the followers of Jesus must live in the context of a secular culture, reinterpreting biblical concepts from within it. Although Bonhoeffer did not live long enough to work out his ideas, he seemed, as John Kent points out,[30] to see the way forward to be a theology of historical adaptation with the 'lordship' of Jesus over all cultures and in relation to the actual historical environment. The central thesis of Bonhoeffer's major work, *The Cost of Discipleship* (1937), is very reminiscent of Kierkegaard in its protest against 'cheap grace' purveyed in the doctrines, rites and institutions of official religion. Like Kierkegaard, Bonhoeffer calls for 'costly grace', a genuine discipleship that is an obedient and exclusive following of Jesus. In the spiritual regeneration that follows, such a life becomes one of grace because the follower of Jesus becomes the 'new man' in Christ. Similarly in Bonhoeffer's *Ethics* (manuscripts written between 1940 and 1943 in Berlin), 'conformation' to Christ occurs, not through efforts 'to become like Jesus', but through the form of Jesus working on us to make us in its own likeness. Although critical of Barth, Bultmann and Tillich, Bonhoeffer clearly also reflects emphases appearing in Kierkegaard's authorship concerning the divine creation of the self through grace in its daily ethical-religious existence as opposed to the false human effort to create the self, whether within or 'without' organized Christianity. While concrete references to Kierkegaard are scattered in Bonhoeffer's writings, he has clearly read deeply in Kierkegaard, and he catches all the urgency of Kierkegaard's comments in *Two Ages* about the quantitative-minded, mass-media age in which the individual, though in a threatened situation, is educated by it to make the leap into the embrace of God.[31] Certainly Bonhoeffer himself provided a living illustration of what it can mean to take the gospel seriously in Kierkegaardian terms.[32]

Notes

1. Johannes Sløk, 'Kierkegaard and Luther' in *A Kierkegaard Critique*, ed. Howard A. Johnson and Niels Thulstrup (New York: Harper & Brothers, 1962), ch. 6, pp. 85–6.

2. H. Roos, *Søren Kierkegaard og Katolicismen: Søren Kierkegaard Selskabets Populære Skrifter* II (Copenhagen: Ejnar Munksgaard, 1952), pp. 53–5.

3. For a detailed discussion of Kierkegaard and Luther see Johannes Sløk, 'Kierkegaard and Luther'; Regin Prenter, 'Luther and Lutheranism' in *Bibliotheca Kierkegaardiana* VI: *Kierkegaard and Great Traditions*, ed. Niels Thulstrup and Marie Mikulová Thulstrup (Copenhagen: C. A. Reitzels Boghandel, 1981), pp. 121–72; Craig Quentin Hinkson, 'Kierkegaard's theology: cross and grace. The Lutheran and Idealist traditions in his thought' (Chicago: PhD in theology, University of Chicago Divinity School, December 1993).

4. PAP, XI,1 A 61, 193, 442, 572, XI,2 A 303 (JP).

5. PAP, I A 101; XI,1 A 237 (JP). This does not mean, however, that Kierkegaard is claiming that Augustine ignores the application of Christianity to existence.

6. SV, IV 297–322, esp. 304, 300 (CA); SV II 194 (EOII).

7. On St Augustine, see Jørgen Pedersen, 'Augustine and Augustinianism' in *Bibliotheca Kierkegaardiana* VI: *Kierkegaard and Great Traditions*, pp. 54–97.

8. Marie Mikulová Thulstrup, *Kierkegaard og Pietismen*: *Søren Kierkegaard Selskabets Populære Skrifter* XIII (Copenhagen: Munksgaards Forlag, 1967), esp. pp. 44–58; also as 'Pietism' in *Bibliotheca Kierkegaardiana* VI: *Kierkegaard and Great Traditions*, pp. 173–222, esp. 209–22.

9. PAP, X,3 A 437, 556 (JP).

10. PAP, X,3 A 174; X,4 A 33 (JP).

11. Kierkegaard refers to writers such as Cyprian, Origen, Irenaeus, Tertullian, Basil, Ambrose, Justin Martyr, Clement of Alexandria, Makarios the Egyptian, John Chrysostom, Thomas Aquinas, Bernard of Clairvaux, Hugh and Richard of St Victor, Francis of Assisi, Thomas à Kempis, Savonarola. Among other names appearing in Kierkegaard's writings can be mentioned, in addition to Augustine and Luther, Anselm, Pascal, Tersteegen and Schleiermacher.

12. PAP, X,3 A 420 (JP).

13. See Louis Dupré, *Kierkegaard as Theologian* (London and New York: Sheed & Ward, 1963), pp. xii, 222–3.

14. Here can be named Kierkegaard's influence on the ultra-conservative Inner Mission Pietist Vilhelm Beck (1829–1901), on the Danish literary critic Georg Brandes (1842-1927) and on the positivist Danish philosopher Harald Høffding (1843–1931). See also Kirmmse, *Golden Age Denmark*, pp. 482–6.

15. Some useful material on the reception of Kierkegaard is to be found in *Bibliotheca Kierkegaardiana* VIII: *The Legacy and Interpretation of Kierkegaard*, ed. Niels Thulstrup and Marie Mikulová Thulstrup (Copenhagen: C. A. Reitzels Boghandel, 1981); also in *Bibliotheca Kierkegaardiana* XV: *Kierkegaard Research*, ed. Niels Thulstrup and Marie Mikulová Thulstrup (Copenhagen: C. A. Reitzels Forlag, 1987); J. Heywood Thomas and Richard Summers, 'British Kierkegaard research: a historical survey', *Kierkegaardiana* 15 (1991), pp. 117–35.

16. Emil Brunner, *Truth as Encounter* (Philadelphia: Westminster, 1964), p. 112. See also Timothy Tian-Min Lin, *The Life and Thought of Søren Kierkegaard* (New Haven, CT: College & University Press, 1974), p. 109.

17. Paul Roubiczek, *Eksistentialismen: En kritisk vurdering* (Copenhagen: Munksgaard, 1968), p. 61; also in *Existentialism: For and Against* (Cambridge: Cambridge University Press, 1964), p. 55. See also Duncan, *Sören Kierkegaard*, p. 114.

18. Ronald Grimsley, *Kierkegaard*, p. 112.

19. On Sartre, see Duncan, *Sören Kierkegaard*, pp. 47–54.

20. See Jean-Paul Sartre, *Existentialism and Humanism* (London: Methuen & Co. Ltd., 1948), esp. pp. 26–30, 34–5, on the themes of existence coming before essence, man's freedom and responsibility.

21. Karl Jaspers, *Philosophy* (Chicago: University of Chicago Press, 1969), 'Epilogue 1955', 1:9; also in Duncan, *Sören Kierkegaard*, p. 117.

22. N. H. Søe, 'Karl Barth' in *Bibliotheca Kierkegaardiana* VIII: *The Legacy and Interpretation of Kierkegaard*, ed. Niels Thulstrup and Marie Mikulová Thulstrup (Copenhagen: C. A. Reitzels Boghandel, 1981), pp. 224–37. Søe gives a detailed presentation of the similarities and differences between Kierkegaard and Barth.

23. Karl Barth, 'A thank you and a bow: Kierkegaard's reveille', translated by H. Martin Rumscheidt, *Canadian Journal of Theology* 11 (1965), 1, pp. 3–7, esp. 6–7. See also Søe, 'Karl Barth', pp. 235–6.
24. PAP, XI,1 A 28 (JP).
25. SV, IX (WL). See also SV VII, fn. p. 484 (CUP); SV XIII, 589–92 (PVMA, pp. 107–10) and PAP, VII,1 A 20; X,2 A 390 (JP).
26. It is, of course, not possible here to deal with all the Christian theologians and thinkers influenced and inspired in any way by Kierkegaard, especially as this unavoidably raises the question of definitions and amounts of influence/inspiration, not least where Kierkegaard is read and criticized – thus becoming, however briefly, even a negative inspiration. A case in point is K. E. Løgstrup in Denmark: see his *Den Etiske Fordring* (Copenhagen: Gyldendal, 1956, 1975) and his *Opgør med Kierkegaard* (Copenhagen: Gyldendal, 1968, 1994).
27. Jørgen K. Bukdahl, 'Bultmann' in *Bibliotheca Kierkegaardiana* VIII: *The Legacy and Interpretation of Kierkegaard*, pp. 238-42.
28. Paul Tillich, *Perspectives on 19th and 20th Century Protestant Theology*, ed. Carl R. Braaten (New York: Harper & Row, 1967), p. 162; see also Duncan, *Sören Kierkegaard*, pp. 128–32.
29. Paul Tillich, *Systematic Theology* (Great Britain: James Nisbet & Co., 1968), I, p. 15.
30. John Kent, *The End of the Line?* (Philadelphia: Fortress Press, 1978, 1982), p. 127. See also John Macquarrie, *Twentieth-Century Religious Thought* (London: SCM Press, 1963, 1976), pp. 330–2.
31. SV, VIII, 101 (TA).
32. See Renate Wind, *A Spoke in the Wheel: The Life of Dietrich Bonhoeffer* (London: SCM Press, 1991).

8

Kierkegaard in an ecumenical perspective

It was on 1 September 1855, in the last number of his paper *The Instant*,[1] that Kierkegaard wrote that his task was the Socratic one of revising the definition of what it meant to be a Christian. Presenting Christianity in its highest ideality and refusing to call himself by the high title of Christian, Kierkegaard made it yet again clear that this task of 'revision' or acting as a 'corrective' was far from any kind of revision or correction of Christian doctrine. On the one hand he aimed to clarify concepts and stir people into taking Christian ideality seriously. On the other, he wished to prick the bubble of 'Christendom', the Golden Age amalgam of Church and State that fostered the illusion that to live Christianly was to view a cosy bourgeois existence as the goal of life.[2] Kierkegaard felt called upon to act as such a corrective to the established order particularly because he saw that the old regulating weight that Christianity once provided – the thought that one had to strive for one's eternal salvation, one's heavenly blessedness, during one's temporal life – had vanished.[3]

The twentieth-century world differs considerably from Kierkegaard's situation. Far from living in a unified, Christian-based culture, we live in the context of a plurality of creeds, unified, if at all, by the world-view of science in its technological application. Whereas in Kierkegaard's time many took their eternal salvation so much for granted they did not feel the need to make any special moral and spiritual effort, in our own century a number of Christians hardly like to be reminded that any ever took the kingdom of heaven as a serious proposition. 'Eternal life' has often been reinterpreted as purely a spiritual quality of temporal life with

Christian emphasis only on social concerns.[4] Despite works like *The Cloud of Unknowing*,[5] the notion of heaven as a destination and goal has often been interpreted by moderns in materialistic terms and ascribed as such to an inadequate medieval world-view incompatible with the findings of modern science.

As we approach the twenty-first century, further developments have included an intensification of doctrinal fundamentalism within major religions, but a more open attitude on the part of science towards people's parapsychological and personal religious experience. An interest in immortality as reincarnation has sprung up within some areas of the Christian tradition, while death is ceasing to be an unspeakable subject. These developments are but some, however, amid a diversity of world-views, life-styles and attitudes, and, given Kierkegaard's Danish Christian cultural background, it has to be asked how he continues to be able to speak successfully to so many in our day.[6] One must remember that, quite apart from his appeal to Christian thinkers from different streams in the main denominations (Catholic, Protestant and Greek and Russian Orthodox), Kierkegaard's thought has also been taken up by scholars and writers in relation to other religions: Judaism, Buddhism and, most recently, Islam.[7] It has also been of importance to figures such as Miguel de Unamuno (1864–1936), Franz Kafka (1883–1924) and Ludwig Wittgenstein (1889–1951). Kierkegaard's psychological insights have long been taken up and applied in psychiatry.[8] At the present time, Kierkegaard is known to be studied and discussed by people from over 60 nations.[9] There are also many Kierkegaard groups and societies all over the world, meeting to discuss subjects covering a broad spectrum of human interests.

I am convinced that the continuing interest in Kierkegaard in the late twentieth century arises from his profound spirituality, coupled with an ability to address undogmatically a multiplicity of interests and interest groups. He is thus able to be a truly ecumenical figure in a pluralistic age, attracting the interest of vastly different disciplines, from religious studies to computer studies and physics. Since he addresses every aspect of human existence and is so Socratic in approach, he is also able to draw together a wide range of different personal perspectives in multicultural dialogue.[10] In his use of the Socratic method, Kierkegaard strove to keep his own view to himself through the use of pseudonyms, acting as an 'occasion' for people's discovery and self-discovery instead of setting himself up as a teaching authority or arguing the rightness of his own ideas. I would urge that it is this feature of Kierkegaard's writing that makes him especially effective in a time when two main tendencies seem to be especially dominant – a pluralism that accepts the personal validity of all views but stands by the correctness of no particular view of the universe, and a scientific or religious fundamentalism that is rigidly exclusive of views other than its own. Kierkegaard avoids the pitfalls of both trends, and he also does something else; he makes room for truth, both intellectual and existential, through encouraging people to be open-minded, to be aware of the spiritual dimension of existence, and to venture in life as well as in thought.

Another difficulty Kierkegaard escapes through his Socratic approach to Christianity is that of being restricted to limiting others to a particular set of religious assumptions. One often meets people who are seriously interested in the spiritual life but who express disappointment with religious orthodoxy and religious institutions. It is suggested that the Church or Churches are not getting across to people in some way. Yet quite apart from the question of personal conviction, clergy and professional religious (monks and nuns) are obliged to work within the confines of their particular creeds. The alternative is to 'demythologize' the scripture, but those who do this often fail to see that they are merely importing a part or parts of a secular belief-system into the context of their religious assumptions, and not, as they suppose, making the religious message relevant to 'facts' known for certain by the modern world. In either case, the religious dialogue is often carried on at a propositional level in relation to religious or religious-secular authority. Doctrinal ecumenical dialogue is therefore carried on with a certain reserve and, where scripture is concerned, people have to face either what appears too often to be nit-picking arguments between scholars or a response to religious questions that involves using the sacred scripture as a source of proof texts for elements of the replies.

Like Kierkegaard, one can see the importance of scholarly Bible and scriptural commentaries[11] and it is also equally clear that clergy and professional religious need to justify their comments with some reference to the basic doctrines and documents of their religion. Suppose, however, that the same thing happened in science. Suppose that instead of applying scientific theory and showing others how to apply it – test it in practice – scientists spoke only on the basis of the authority of old textbooks and met at conferences to discuss how such textbooks should be interpreted. Would science then have made the strides it has? The main difference between the two situations is, of course, that testing of scientific theories does not have such a direct effect on personal life. It is one thing to carry out research repeating an experiment on some rare virus and another to try some of the stricter injunctions of the New Testament. Yet the scientists who speak with authority are not necessarily those with official backing from some institution, they are those who speak from personal experience. That is, they actually practise science as opposed to merely talking about it or talking about past scientific discoveries. According to the New Testament, Jesus spoke on the basis of his living experience of God, and his precepts come from this experience. There are also many accounts of the lives of those who did go and do likewise, did follow the precepts of the New Testament and who also report a living experience of God.[12] To this it can be objected that science is carried out on the basis of clearly stated axioms and formulae that anyone can repeat, whereas an injunction such as 'Make love your aim'[13] is an abstract concept that can be understood in a variety of ways. Scripture texts can also be textually unclear. Kierkegaard argues against this that the situation of scholarship (objectivity) is in any case different from that of personal experience (subject-ivity), where one tries out, or lives by, the precepts. He indicates that the situation of the one undertaking the historical-critical method of textual criticism as a substitute for trying out the scrip-tural precepts resembles the situation of scientists talking about science instead of practising it. To attempt to carry out New Testament precepts would be like actually doing science.[14] That the concrete action of altruistic love in practice can be carried out in a number of ways would, on the analogy, be no different to the fact that science can be carried out in a number of ways. Kierkegaard also argues that because some texts in the New Testament may be difficult or obscure, this is no excuse for not trying to live by what one does understand, if one accepts that Christianity has any kind of a claim on one. He urges this in one of his final works, *For Self-Examination* (1851), where he makes clear the essential distinction between the situation of scholarship (objectivity) and the situation of personal experience (subjectivity). He says:

Imagine a lover who has received a letter from his beloved – I assume that God's Word is just as precious to you as this letter is to the lover. I assume that you read and think you ought to read God's Word in the same way the lover reads this letter.

Yet you perhaps say, 'Yes, but Holy Scripture is written in a foreign language.' But it is really only scholars who need to read Holy Scripture in the original language. If, however, you will not have it any other way, if you insist upon reading Scripture in the original language, well, we can still keep the metaphor of the letter from the beloved, except that we will add a little stipulation.

I assume, then, that this letter from the beloved is written in a language that the lover does not understand, and there is no one around who can translate it for him, and perhaps he would not even want any such help lest a stranger be initiated into his secrets. What does he do? He takes a dictionary, begins to spell his way through the letter, looks up every word in order to obtain a translation. Let us assume that, as he sits there busy with his task, an acquaintance comes in. He knows that this letter has come, because he sees it on the table, sees it lying there, and says, 'Well, so you are reading a letter from your beloved' – what do you think the other will say? He answers, 'Have you gone mad? Do you think this is reading a letter from my beloved! No, my friend, I am sitting here toiling and moiling with a dictionary to get it translated. At times I am ready to explode with impatience; the blood rushes to my head and I would just as soon hurl the dictionary on the floor – and you call that reading – you must be joking! No, thank God, I am soon finished with the translation and then, yes then, I shall read my beloved's letter; that is something altogether different.'[15]

Kierkegaard goes on to describe the possibility that the letter contained something the beloved wanted the recipient to do, and that the recipient, thanks to a mistranslation and misunderstanding of the text, rushed off and did the wrong thing and found out only later when he encountered the letter-writer. He considers it is better to make a mistake about action than to waste enormous amounts of time – perhaps using up all one's time and ending up not doing anything much. Kierkegaard therefore urges the Bible scholar not to forget to read the Bible and refuses to listen to the plea of the obscurity of some passages from a person who has not first done what is easy to understand, even if there is only one thing that is easy to understand. The kind of mistake Kierkegaard seems to be thinking of here is if, for example, someone sold everything and joined an enclosed religious order, whereas God had really intended that person to exercise Christianity through marriage and ordinary community relationships. That Abraham prepares to obey God concerning the sacrifice of Isaac in the Bible version of the story (Genesis 22:8) can be seen as an indication of his faith that God would really provide a sheep for the sacrifice. The prior question (where people do undertake monstrous deeds thinking it is God's will) is how far a person is really godly in the sense of modelling his or her life on the pattern of the totally altruistic God Kierkegaard describes. That catastrophes such as that of the Pastor Jim Jones group in Guyana do occur cannot be used to discredit authentic religious life and experience, any more than the event of a crooked police-officer or an incompetent doctor can be used to discredit the honest police officer and the competent medic, let alone the entire fields of law and medicine.

Kierkegaard spoke from the depths of his own spiritual experience. He also saw the need for taking the New Testament seriously in its stricter injunctions. Most importantly, he saw the need to treat Christianity as a personal existential adventure in which one is not afraid to risk oneself. So much did he have the courage of this conviction that, far from clinging to scriptural 'proofs', he was fearlessly able to mount a rousing defence of Christianity that seemed to his contemporaries, as he realized it would,[16] more like an attack. He presupposes that the religious 'scientific experiment', though not without risk, will always work if carried through. That is, if one ventures on the basis of love and ethics into a serious God-relationship that also takes the needs of others seriously, a result will emerge for the one who embarked on the venture of faith. Of course it is always possible to make objections to his position, but not reasonably without testing the truth of Kierkegaard's assumption for oneself, by venturing to live for the idea as one understands its claim on one, from the New Testament or one's sacred scripture.

Notes

1. *The Instant* (*Øieblikket*) is to be found in SV, XIV (AC).
2. PAP, XI,2 A 19; X,3 A 565; X,4 A 15 (JP); SV, XIV, pp. 119–20 (AC, p. 97).
3. PAP, XI,1 A 252 (JP).
4. See John Hick, *Death and Eternal Life* (London: Collins, 1976), chs 4 and 5, esp. pp. 92–3. Hick sees post-Second-World-War Christian theology as in disarray in the face of cultural rejection of belief in personal immortality. Such rejection he sees as due to a general assumption that one should believe only what one experiences and what the accredited sciences affirm to be truth.

5. *The Cloud of Unknowing*, chs 51–62, esp. chs 60–61.
6. That he also predicted and attacked the phenomenon of the unthinking masses and the abuse of the mass-media is not a sufficient reason (though it has been given by some readers of Kierkegaard), for other writers, such as Aldous Huxley, have done the same.
7. In Judaism one can think of Martin Buber (1878–1965): see Robert L. Perkins, 'A philosophic encounter with Buber' in *Bibliotheca Kierkegaardiana* VIII: *The Legacy and Interpretation of Kierkegaard*, pp. 243–75. Kierkegaard has also been taken up in Shinran Buddhism: see Olof G. Lidin, *Japans Religioner* (Copenhagen: Politikens Forlag, 1985), p. 136. Safet Bektovic has written about Kierkegaard in relation to Islam: 'Kierkegaard og Islam', in the Danish paper *Information* (2–3 April 1994).
8. For example, R. D. Laing, *The Divided Self* (Harmondsworth: Penguin Books, 1965, 1969), found Kierkegaard's insights about despair fruitful.
9. This can be seen from the nationality and standpoints of writers and translators of Kierkegaard, from the membership of Kierkegaard societies and, finally, from the number and nationality of subscribers to Kierkegaard newsletters and journals.
10. To take but one instance, from February 1980 to December 1993, thanks to Grethe Kjær, international Kierkegaard coffee evenings were regularly held in Copenhagen, Denmark. These crossed all boundaries, disciplinary, cultural and denominational, and were truly ecumenical (including people of religiously agnostic and atheistic standpoints), consisting as they did of friends coming together in free discussion of topics dealt with by Kierkegaard in his writings.
11. SV, VII, p. 15 (CUP); cf. SV, XII, p. 318 (FSE/JY).
12. From Kierkegaard's own time one can mention Jean Vianney (1786–1859), the curé of Ars in France.
13. 1 Cor 14:1.
14. Scholarship applied to Scripture is, of course, perfectly valid as a scientific approach. Within the discipline of textual criticism applied to the Bible the contrast would be between talking about the findings of past Bible scholars and actually carrying out fresh scholarship.
15. SV, XII, pp. 316–22 (FSE/JY); cf. PAP, XI,2 A 51 (JP).
16. PAP, X,2 A 163 (JP).

Index